A Spirituality for Sunday People

Year B

Fr. Kevin E. Mackin, OFM

WESTBOW
PRESS®
A DIVISION OF THOMAS NELSON
& ZONDERVAN

WestBow Press books may be ordered through booksellers or by contacting:

WestBow Press
A Division of Thomas Nelson & Zondervan
1663 Liberty Drive
Bloomington, IN 47403
www.westbowpress.com
1 (866) 928-1240

Cover photo of Fr. Kevin: credit T. Allan Smith

ISBN: 978-1-5127-7188-6 (sc)
ISBN: 978-1-5127-7190-9 (hc)
ISBN: 978-1-5127-7189-3 (e)

Library of Congress Control Number: 2017900413

Print information available on the last page.

WestBow Press rev. date: 2/2/2017

Dedicated to two faithful disciples of Jesus,
my parents,
Martin and Margaret Mackin

Contents

Foreword

Spirituality is "in" these days. There's a wide variety of books, articles, and programs about the quest for an authentic spiritual life.

What is spirituality? It is growing into our lives with God. It is letting the Breath or Spirit of God live, breathe, and work in us. And the fruits of that are "love joy, peace, patience, kindness, generosity, faithfulness, gentleness, self-control" (Gal. 5:22–23).

There are many different spiritual pathways. In Catholic Christianity, these include Benedictine, Franciscan, Dominican, Carmelite, Jesuit, Ursuline, priestly, lay, and so on. But all these are different responses to one common call to holiness. The goal, to paraphrase the Broadway musical *Godspell*, is to see Thee, O Lord, more clearly, love Thee more dearly, and follow Thee more nearly day by day. And we attempt to do this in our own unique way and circumstances.

As a Franciscan priest, I enjoy and propose that we nourish our life with God through the Sunday readings in the Liturgy of the Word. In many ways, we are a Sunday people. We gather every weekend in houses of worship around the globe to praise and thank God in the Liturgy of the Word and the Eucharist. The Word proclaimed Sunday after Sunday is inspired by God. As Mother Teresa put it, "God speaks to us; we listen. We speak to God; He listens."

There are different levels of meaning in the Word in which God speaks, and we hear. Take the wedding at Cana. On one level, Jesus, his mother, and the disciples were simply invited to a local wedding. Mary, in some ways, could have passed for a wedding planner. And there was an embarrassing shortage of wine. Mary may even have indicated to the waiters something like, "See that handsome man there? That's my son; do whatever he says."

On another level, Mary appears as our mediator, interceding with her Son on our behalf. And that is why the Catholic Christian heritage gives a special place of honor to Mary. On a third level, the water made into wine symbolizes the breaking in of the kingdom of God— the symbolic wedding banquet at the End Times with fine wines and delicious food. And on a fourth level, this sign is one of seven pointing to Jesus as the Revelation of God to us.

The point is, God can speak to us on many levels when we are attentive to that word. This is especially so with the word proclaimed to us on Sundays. God is the author of that word in the sense that it contains what God want us to know about him, his relationship with the universe, and his purpose for us. But the authors of the word were real authors, using the languages, images, literary forms, and understandings of God and the world with which they were familiar.

God inspired them to write the truth about him and our relationship to him, but the way they expressed these, and the language and concepts they used to communicate them, remained their own. At the heart of this understanding is the belief that Jesus, the incarnate Word of God, entered into our history and fully embraced our humanity with all its limitations, even to the point of death. In a similar fashion, the Bible is the incarnated word of God, communicated through human authors with their particular world views and limitations.

By reflecting on the word proclaimed over the three-year cycle, I have written this collection of homilies in hopes of touching the hearts and minds of disciples of Jesus who have already heard the call to holiness.

Finally, every author owes indebtedness to certain people, especially for their attention to detail. I am particularly indebted to Janet Gianopoulos, whose invaluable assistance lightened the challenge of publishing this book. A deep and lasting sense of gratitude goes to her.

Fr. Kevin E. Mackin, OFM

First Sunday in Advent

Over the Thanksgiving holidays, I was visiting with family. A relative of mine invited a number of people to dinner. At the table, she turned to their little daughter and said, "Would you like to say the blessing?"

Her daughter replied, "I don't know what to say."

"Just say what you've heard Mommy say," the mother answered.

And the little girl bowed her head and said, "Lord, why on earth did I invite so many people to dinner?"

At another gathering, I overheard a boy praying this: "Lord, if you can't make me a better person, don't worry about it. I'm having a real good time like I am."

These are the types of amusing, bemusing, and touching comments one hears at a large family table.

Many people seem to be searching for the secret to happiness, especially during the holiday season. Someone wrote that all it takes to be happy is the ability to do the following: forgive, apologize (we all make mistakes), and move on; listen to advice; keep your temper; share the blame; make the best out of the situation (most things in life seldom work out perfectly); and put the needs of others before your own desires. If we practice these secrets to happiness, we'll soon have a more positive outlook on life.

That's what Advent is all about—hope in the future, a glorious future in which we will be transformed into a new heavenly reality, like Jesus before us. And so we pray during the Advent season, "Come, Lord Jesus, and fashion us, like the potter with clay, into new creatures." "Come, Lord Jesus" is the so-called Maranatha Prayer in the last chapter of the book of Revelation.

As we reflect on global, economic, political, and natural turmoil, some people may feel the sentiments of the great twentieth-century Irish poet William Butler Yeats, who wrote in his poem "The Second Coming,"

> Things fall apart; the centre cannot hold;
> Mere anarchy is loosed upon the world,
> The blood dimm'd tide is loosed, and everywhere
>
> The ceremony of innocence is drowned;
>
> The best lack all convictions, while the worst
> Are full of passionate intensity.

Advent speaks loudly and clearly against these sentiments. It invites us and welcomes us to reflect on the threefold coming of Jesus. He came to us centuries ago in Bethlehem of Judea. He comes to us now sacramentally in the signs of bread and wine, and he will come again triumphantly and gloriously at the End Times.

And so, in addition to liturgies, how might we celebrate Advent this year? Some families create an Advent wreath with four candles and light one candle at the dinner table during the first week, two candles during the second week, and so on. After lighting the candle, they pray in their own words for the coming of the Messiah into their own lives. Other families make a Jesse Tree to experience the story of our salvation as told in the Hebrew Bible. Still other families might set up a Nativity scene and invite family members to take turns telling, in their own words, the meaning of Christmas at the family dinner table. These are but a few family customs that can help keep alive the meaning of Advent. In the larger parish family, we might engage in volunteer service activities.

The word of God takes us back in our imaginations to the sixth century before Jesus to a man by the name of Isaiah, also known as "third Isaiah." The author acknowledged how the Hebrews often broke their covenant with God through their many infidelities. He described graphically who they are—mere clay in the imaginative hands of God, their maker or potter. The author then prayed that God, who worked mighty signs and awesome wonders in the past, would reappear to the Hebrews now, as he did at Mount Sinai centuries before, and would find them doing good. That prayer might well be ours too: for God to appear and find us doing good.

In his letter to the Christian community in Corinth in Greece, Paul prayed that God would bestow his gifts of grace and peace on the community. And as they waited for the revelation or appearance of our Lord Jesus Christ, Paul prayed that God would help them stay the course. Surely Paul's prayer is ours as well.

In the Gospel according to Mark, the author challenged us to always be alert and watchful for the Lord's coming. (Mark 13) Always should we live lives worthy of our calling as sons and daughters of God.

The Advent season is really about waiting. We do plenty of waiting, don't we? We wait in line to purchase an item. We wait in an office to see a doctor. Yes, we do a lot of waiting. So, too, did folks in scripture, but theirs was a different kind of waiting. They often waited for the Messiah to rescue them from their hardships, the follies of their kings, their exile, and their sufferings throughout their many foreign occupations. And yet the Messiah often seemed to be hidden.

We, too, often pray to God to rescue us from a crisis of one kind or another. We beg God to suddenly appear and make things right for us. Some would say this is the story of everyone. Where was God when a loved one was in harm's way? Why didn't God protect him or her? There are no answers that satisfy us. Yes, we pray for God to rescue us, and yet God can seem silent, hidden from our eyes. But is God silent? Is God hidden?

We profess that God is indeed in our midst, not in a manger. That event happened centuries ago in Bethlehem. Where is God today? All around us. In nature, in a sunrise and sunset, in a landscape and waterscape, in people, and in our beloved pets. God is with us as we ache with all sorts of growing pains and groan in prayer during times of a life-threatening illness, a broken relationship, or a job loss, for example. He is especially within the word proclaimed and the sacraments. Yes, we mystically encounter the living Christ, body and blood, soul and divinity.

Saint Paul wrote that God's favor, his grace, has been revealed to us in Jesus. (1 Cor. 1:3-9) And so we wait and sing, "O Come, Emmanuel," God with us. Jesus has been transformed into a new, heavenly reality that one day will be ours as well, and we are called to continue the saving work of Jesus Christ.

Let us pray this Advent season that the Spirit of God, who overshadowed the Virgin Mary and brought forth the word made flesh, will reenergize us to become better instruments of faith in God, hope in eternal life, and love for one another. May we be better channels of forgiveness, compassion, truth, and fairness; and better companions in hospitality, service, and responsibility until Jesus Christ comes again in glory.

Second Sunday in Advent

My doctor just told me I have an Advent virus, and people can catch it very quickly. Does anyone else have this Advent virus? Here are some signs and symptoms: frequent attacks of smiling; frequent, overwhelming episodes of appreciation of others; a loss of interest in judging other people negatively; an inability to worry; and an uncontrollable urge to reach out to others with a helping hand. If you have some of these symptoms, that's good.

On this second Sunday of Advent, the word of God takes us to the sixth century before Jesus to a man named Isaiah. The author spoke about a fresh start, new beginnings, for the Hebrews. They were free at last from their exile in Babylonia—modern Iraq—free at last to go back to their homeland to rebuild their lives. George Handel's *Messiah*, with its soaring "Hallelujah Chorus," immortalizes this passage: "Comfort ye, my people." And of course Dr. Martin Luther King, Jr., speaking of his dream, revived forever the phrase "free at last."

Yes, scripture challenges us to begin every day with a fresh start in our lives of discipleship with Jesus. The second letter of Peter describes in apocalyptic images—fire, wind, and earthquakes—the future, a new heaven, and a new earth. Until Jesus comes again in glory, the author begged the members of the community to live each day as though it were their last, for Jesus may come suddenly and unexpectedly to ask about our lives. Yes, that message is for us.

In the Gospel according to Mark, John the Baptist appeared in the wilderness, proclaiming repentance: "Prepare the way for the Lord."

(Mark 1:1-8) That is the mission: repent and orient our lives to God and to one another. That's what Advent is all about—preparing for Christ by reorienting our lives.

During Advent the word of God focuses on three biblical personalities: Isaiah, John the Baptist, and the Virgin Mary. All three, in their experience of God, delivered a special message. Isaiah spoke about a future Messiah, a liberator, a redeemer, and a savior for us. John the Baptist pointed to Jesus as the Lamb of God. The lamb, of course, references the Hebrew Passover meal, the seder Jews celebrate to this very day. Jesus is the Lamb who through his own death and resurrection created a future for us, transforming us into a new heavenly reality. The Virgin Mary is the living temple of God, the ark of the Hebrew covenant, because she carried within herself the presence of God; the Word made flesh; a child, Emmanuel, which means "God with us."

The word of God also references a fourth biblical personality, Joseph, who appears ever so briefly in Advent and then disappears. Joseph had a dream in which the angel said, "Do not be afraid to take Mary as your wife." (Matthew 1:20) As I thought about Joseph's dream, I wondered about what couples dream when they learn they will be parents. They usually begin to dream about their child. Their first dreams are usually for a safe birth, a healthy child. Then parents may dream that their son or daughter will excel in sports, master the sciences, or distinguish himself or herself in the arts, music, or literature. They may even dream that their child may one day be a star quarterback for the Tampa Bay Buccaneers, a singer at the Met, or a mover and shaker in politics.

But along the way, of course, dreams may change very quickly. While they once dreamed about the Nobel Prize, Mom and Dad may now settle for their child passing courses in biology, math, or literature. Their dream of a World Series baseball champion may be forgotten when they wait and hope their child will recover from an illness or an auto accident. Their dream of a Bill Gates-like genius may all but disappear when they pray that their child will overcome an addiction of one kind or another.

As I think of Joseph's dreams, I also think of the dreams of so many people. Sometimes disappointments, so-called bad luck, or tragedy may change our dreams. But as Joseph learned from his dreams, the most important things we can dream for children are the following:

- That they always will know that we love them dearly
- That we accept them unconditionally for who they are
- That we are always ready to forgive them for their so-called peccadilloes (as I hope they are ready to forgive ours)
- And that we are always praying that God will grace them with his gifts

Like Joseph, let us pray for the grace to see God's presence in all things, especially in ordinary things; to do things as best we can; to accept people as a gift from God, even if they're not quite the gift we hoped for; and to be a source of affirmation and support.

I close with a few lines of a favorite poem about an old, battered violin up for auction. The story changes course when someone wipes the dust from the violin, tightens the loose strings, and plays an angelic melody. Then the bidding soars.

> And many a person with life out of tune
> And battered and scarred with sin
> Is auctioned cheap to the thoughtless crowd,
> Much like the old violin …
>
> But the Master comes, and the foolish crowd
> Never can quite understand
> The worth of the soul and the change that's wrought
> By the touch of the Master's hand.

As we prepare for the birth of the eternal Word of God at Christmas, let us pray that the touch of the Master's hand will change us into ever-more faithful disciples of Jesus. And may the touch of our hands be channels of grace to those whose lives are out of tune this season.

Third Sunday in Advent

I don't know about you, but I'm feeling a bit tired these days, and it's not even Christmas yet. But then I figured it out. I found the data. An adult of average weight, does the following each day:

- Your heart beats over 103,000 times.
- And your blood travels 168,000,000 miles.
- You breathe over 23,000 times, and inhale almost 440 cubic feet of air.
- You eat pounds of food and drink quarts of liquids. You speak 25,000 words.
- You move 750 muscles. And you exercise 7,000,000 brain cells.

Now that's work. No wonder we might feel tired.

Christmas is only eleven days away, and Christmas carols can be heard all around. How many know the "The Twelve Days of Christmas"? Do you know the story behind that carol? For some two centuries, Catholics in England couldn't practice their faith openly. Remember Saint Thomas More in the movie *A Man for All Seasons*? He was a person who stood for integrity.

"The Twelve Days of Christmas" is a statement about Catholic belief. The carol has two levels of meaning.

- The partridge in a pear tree is Christ.
- The two turtle-doves are the New and Old Testaments.

- The three French hens stand for faith, hope, and love.
- The four calling birds are the four Gospels.
- The five golden rings refer to the Torah or the first five books of the Hebrew Bible.
- The six geese a-laying stand for the six days of creation.
- The seven swans a-swimming represent the seven gifts of the Spirit.
- The eight maids a-milking are the eight beatitudes.
- The nine ladies dancing are the nine fruits of the spirit.
- The ten lords a-leaping are the Ten Commandments.
- The eleven pipers piping stand for the eleven faithful disciples.
- And the twelve drummers drumming symbolize the twelve points of belief in the Apostles' Creed.

So if you are singing "The Twelve Days of Christmas" during the holiday season, you might test your religious education or the education of children or grandchildren.

The Advent season invites us to reflect on the threefold coming of Jesus. The child Jesus came to us centuries ago, the living Christ (body and blood, soul and divinity) comes to us now sacramentally and mystically, and Christ will come again gloriously at the End Times.

This Sunday is known as Gaudete Sunday (*Gaudete* is a Latin word that means "rejoice"). We rejoice because we are midway in our Advent journey and because Christ, God's anointed, the Messiah, will soon come at Christmas.

The word of God, just proclaimed, takes us back to the sixth century before Jesus to the Hebrews who were resettling in their devastated homeland after their exile in ancient Babylonia. Ruin and debris were everywhere, yet the prophet proclaimed good news (in other words, healing, freedom, favor, and justice). Jerusalem, like a garden, would come to life again.

Ultimately the good news is Jesus—the Word made flesh. The prophet might ask us, "What kind of good news or message do we bring to people?"

In his letter to the Christian community at Thessalonica in Greece, Paul urged us to rejoice always, pray continuously, and give thanks to

God. "Count your blessings," Paul said. And then he prayed that God would make the community holy. We pray a similar prayer. And in the Gospels, John the Baptizer announced that he was the "voice" in the wilderness who prepared the way for the Messiah. John was the "witness" who pointed to Jesus.

To whom and what do our lifestyle and behavior point? Jesus? Or something else?

Three personalities dominate the scriptures during the Advent season: Isaiah, John the Baptizer, and the Virgin Mary. Today I would like to reflect on John the Baptist.

John is called the "Baptist" because he immersed people in the waters of the Jordan River as a sign of cleansing from old ways so they could live in fidelity to God's covenant. John was the forerunner of Jesus, the one who prepared the way for Jesus, the bridge between two covenants that created a special relationship between God and us: that of the Hebrews and that of Jesus Christ. John wasn't into fashion and gourmet food; he lived a rugged, ascetic lifestyle, dressing simply in camel skin and eating locusts and wild honey.

His message was very simple. He proclaimed what the prophet Micah had begged the Hebrews to do centuries before: do what is right, love goodness, and walk humbly with God. "Repent," John cried out. "Orient your life to God's covenant."

John pointed to Jesus as the Light, the Lord, the One to whom we owe our ultimate allegiance, the Passover or sacrificial Lamb of God, through whose blood we have God's friendship and eternal life again.

John was indeed the herald of Jesus; and for speaking the truth to King Herod, John was imprisoned and executed. He inspires and challenges us to be heralds of Jesus in our families, workplaces, and communities by the manner in which we live. That is how we prepare the way for the Lord.

The Gospel sums up John's mission in the song of Zechariah, John's father. "For you will go before the Lord to prepare his ways." (Luke 1:76) We are called to prepare the way of the Lord so he can enter into the hearts of our fellow human beings and so that through our own hearts, the grace and favor of God can empower others to do what is right, love goodness and walk humbly with God. There's no better place to begin preparing the Lord's way than in our own families. And how do we prepare the way for the Lord in our own families?

First, try to create a better sense of togetherness, of closeness and care for one another. Keep in touch, even if it's only by telephone, e-mail, or Skype; be hospitable and concerned about elderly grandparents or relatives. Remember birthdays or anniversaries and celebrate them together, if possible. Participate in special events—for example, graduations, baptisms, confirmations, marriages, Sunday liturgies, and cookouts. Communicate, take responsibility for family chores, spend time with one another, share the good news as well as the bad; keep your word and thereby build up trust with one another.

Second, strengthen your family life. There are so many activities that can divide a family; activities are valuable in themselves, but if not checked, they can rob families of time together. And finally, parents need to help children become the persons God created them to be. The purpose of family is to provide a secure and loving environment until children become mature enough to venture out on their own as responsible persons.

So like John the Baptizer, we are called to prepare the way for the Lord, especially in our own families. Why not begin by creating an even better sense of togetherness, by spending more time together, and by cherishing more deeply all for who they are?

Fourth Sunday in Advent

Christmas in one sense is a children's festival. So I found a collection of first-grader versions of well-known proverbs or maxims. Here's how the kids put some of the sayings:

> Children should be seen and not spanked or grounded.
> You can't teach an old dog new Math.
> A bird in the hand is going to poop on you.
> Where there's smoke, there's pollution.

You may want to ask your youngsters to complete your favorite proverbs. They may surprise you.

Santa Claus is popping up everywhere, so I also found a Santa story. Santa said to a couple of parents and grandparents, "Teach your children the true meaning of Christmas." He reached into his bag and pulled out a fir tree. "Teach your children that the fir tree's green color symbolizes hope, and so always hope or trust in God; and the needles on the fir tree point heavenward, so every day think about the presence of God in your own life."

Santa again reached into his bag, pulled out a brilliant star, and said, "The star symbolizes the fulfillment of God's promise of a Savior. So keep your promises."

He then pulled out a candle. "The candle symbolizes Christ, the Light of the world, who scatters the darkness all around us." So as you go about your daily routine, ask yourself, "What would Jesus do?"

Santa then pulled out an ornament of himself. "Santa symbolizes generosity and good will. So be generous with what you have and think positively about people."

Santa then hung a candy cane on the tree. "The candy cane symbolizes a shepherd's staff which helps to bring strayed sheep back. So become your 'brother's keeper.'"

He reached in once more, pulled out an angel, and said, "Teach your children that the angels sang the glorious news of the Savior's birth." So be a good finder. Look for the good in yourself, in other people, and in every situation in life. Yes, these symbols associated with Santa Claus can invite us to reflect on the true meaning of Christmas and bow down, like the shepherds or the wise men, to worship Christ, Emmanuel, God with us.

The author of the Santa story is unknown, but the story of Christmas is right in scriptures.

The word of God carries us back in our imaginations three thousand years ago to the days of King David in Jerusalem. David's life in many ways was a soap opera. He was a man of virtue as well as vice.

David wanted to build a temple for the ark of the covenant, a symbol of God's presence. And the prophet Nathan through an oracle said that everything David had was a gift from God. After all, David had once herded sheep, and now he was a king.

Then the prophet proclaimed that God would build a house for David, a dynasty that would endure forever, an heir, an allusion to the Messiah. The author challenges us, as he challenged David, to give thanks to God for all we have.

When I think of gratitude, I recall a Franciscan soup kitchen, St. Francis Inn. As one of our friars describes it, on a cold and rainy Philadelphia night, people were crowding into the big dining room in shifts of fifty at a time.

In came an old woman, with all her possessions in three shopping bags. She ate a sandwich and sipped soup until the bowl was empty. And then she disappeared into the night. When the friar cleaned up, beneath the bowl were four pennies. She had left a tip. As little as she had, this old woman, a "bag lady," knew the meaning of gratitude. This is a powerful reminder to all of us to be grateful, especially during the Christmas season.

Paul, in his letter to the Christian community in Rome, sang a hymn of praise. Paul, a devout Jew, said God's special favor (in other words Jesus Christ) had come through ancient Israel to all people, Jews as well as Gentiles. And to God alone we owe worship. Paul challenged us to recognize who we are: fragile, mortal creatures in the presence of an awesome God, to whom we are accountable for what we do.

In the Gospel according to Luke we have the Annunciation. Somehow the power of God broke into the life of Mary at Nazareth, asking Mary to believe she would bear within herself a special child. Mary was so attuned to the presence of God, such a woman of faith, that she said simply, "May it be done to me according to your word." (Luke 1:26-38)

These words are easy to say when everything is going our way, but they aren't so easy when what is happening is the opposite of what we want to happen. Perhaps there is something we wanted but now won't have: a particular promotion. Perhaps there is a broken relationship, an unexpected illness. Such turns in life can test our trust in God.

But Mary's yes gave us the Christmas story, the world's greatest love story. That story, as it has come down to us, tells of a baby in a trough. It tells of a mother holding her child in her arms as her husband Joseph stayed near. It tells of angels singing in the sky and shepherds running over the hillside to tell the child how much they loved him. Yes, it tells of a star guiding magi over the wilderness and onto their knees to worship.

Centuries ago Saint John summed up this greatest love story in a single line: "The Word became flesh." Yes, John wrote for us, "In the beginning was the word and the word was with God and the word was God. Through him all things came to be and apart from him nothing came to be. He was the light that shines in the darkness and the darkness did not overcome it. And the word became flesh and made his dwelling among us." (John 1:14)

Christmas means not simply God in Bethlehem centuries ago but God within us today. We bear within ourselves Emmanuel, God with us, by virtue of the waters of baptism whenever we gather together in his name before the word of God and around the table of the Lord, the altar. Paul summed this up magnificently centuries ago. We are by grace what Jesus Christ is by nature: sons and daughters of God. That is God's gift to us.

I close with a thought from a little story by O. Henry, "The Gift of the Magi." It's about a young married couple, almost penniless. Della sells her hair to buy a gift for Jim. Jim's present to her is a set of expensive combs for her hair. And her gift to Jim? A chain for his grandfather's watch, which he had sold to buy her combs. But both are happy.

O. Henry concluded with this quote: "Two foolish children who most unwisely sacrificed for each other the greatest treasures they had. But of all who give and receive gifts, such as they are wisest. Everywhere they are wisest. They are the magi."

May we this Christmas, like the magi, bring to the Christ child our greatest gifts: ourselves and our commitment to a life of deeper discipleship with Jesus.

Christmas

In anticipation of the Christmas holidays, a young couple in Florida I knew invited me to their home for dinner. While they were in the kitchen, I asked their son what we were having for dinner. The youngster replied, "Goat."

I said, "Goat?" Are you sure?"

"Yep," he said. "Daddy said to mommy, 'Today is as good as any to have the old goat for dinner.'"

We had chicken Francese!

Every year we relive the wonderful Christmas story. The story tells us of a baby in a trough, of a mother holding her child in her arms as her husband Joseph stayed near, of angels singing, and of shepherds running over the hillside to tell the child they loved him.

The Gospel according to John sums up this magnificent story in a single line: "The Word became flesh." That single line takes us back in our imaginations to the beginning of the human family in Genesis: when man and woman walked with God and had friendship with God and one another. But somehow the man and woman lost that friendship; they fell from grace. Genesis describes that fall very simply yet powerfully. They hid from God, one blamed another, and even the earthly elements worked against them.

But God didn't leave us to ourselves. Remember the words of the prophet Isaiah. "Can a woman forget her infant…Even should she forget, I will never forget you." (Isaiah 49:15) And so continued the story known as our salvation.

In the midst of all ancient Israel's triumphs and tragedies, fortunes and misfortunes, fidelities and infidelities to the covenant, God never reneged on his promises. And so the Word became flesh and made his dwelling among us.

The word of God for the Christmas liturgies is like a prism through which is refracted the multiple facets of this great mystery of the incarnation. Isaiah proclaimed glad tidings: the people who walked in darkness have seen a great light. (Isaiah 9:1-16) Paul wrote that the grace of God appeared in Jesus Christ, who made us heirs to the promise of eternal life.

In the Gospel according to Luke, we read that the Virgin Mary gave birth to her Son. She wrapped him in swaddling clothes and laid him in a manger. And the Gospel of John sums up the meaning of Christmas: "The Word became flesh." That is God's greatest gift to us.

Some of us may be stressed out from holiday shopping and wondering whether a so-called perfect gift is really what someone needs or even wants. Marian Wright Edelman, the children's advocate and author, got it right when she wrote that the best presents she received as a child weren't wrapped in pretty boxes or found under the Christmas tree.

From her father, she received the gift of a love of reading. For him, books to improve the mind were more important than buying toys. From her mother, young Marian received the gift of a passion for children's rights. As a child, her mother asked her to share her room with a child whose own parents weren't able to care for the child. This was one of nearly a dozen foster brothers and sisters her mother raised. And from a neighbor, young Marian received the gift of courage not to be afraid of anything when something important or good just had to be done. She wrote in her autobiography, *Lanterns: A Memoir of Mentors*, "I carry with me and treasure the lessons in life my parents and caring neighbors gave me throughout my childhood. And may these memories give me the strength to give a child a true gift—time spent with them, time spent sharing some of the great lives of mentors who have enriched, informed and helped shape my life."

The point is that there are some gifts that really can transform the lives of people. These are the gifts of teaching, of listening and supporting, of sharing time and experiences, of compassion and forgiveness and affirmation. And this kind of gift giving begins in our own families, workplaces, and communities. These are enduring gifts we can always give to one another: gifts that can transform lives.

Now let's go back to Christmas and the phrase that magnificently sums it up. "The Word became flesh." That single line changed our destiny forever. Christmas means not simply God in Bethlehem of Judea centuries ago but God within us. We carry within ourselves Emmanuel, God with us. How? By virtue of the life-giving waters of baptism.

We gather to proclaim the awesome Word of God, to celebrate the presence of the living Christ, body and blood, soul and divinity, in this liturgy. For we are by grace what Jesus Christ is by nature: sons and daughters of God, heirs to the kingdom of God. And that great truth of our faith, God within us, ought to challenge us always to be good finders: those who look for the good in themselves, in other people, and in every situation.

Look for the good in yourself. Remember that magnificent hymn of the Virgin Mary: "My soul proclaims the greatness of the Lord; my spirit rejoices in God my savior for he has looked upon his lowly servant. From this day all generations will call me blessed: the Almighty has done great things for me, and holy is his name." (Luke 1:46-49) Mary rejoiced in the gifts God gave her, and so too should we rejoice in the gifts God has given us.

Second, look for the good in other people. Someone wrote that people in many ways are like wild flowers. If you have ever studied a wild flower carefully, you saw the delicate veins, the fragile petals, the beautiful blossom. If you turned the flower to the sunlight, you discovered its special symmetry. The wild flower has a beauty all its own, and so do people. And finally look for good in all situations of life. When one door closes, another door inevitably opens if we pay close enough attention.

Who is the ultimate good finder. God so loved us that he became one of us. Yes, Jesus had a unique relationship. He was one with God. He is a God-man: a healer, teacher, and peacemaker. Think of all the people in the Gospels Jesus met: the blind, the leper, the lame, the sinner, and the forgotten. And Jesus found goodness in all of them where many didn't.

The promised Messiah has come. He is in our midst sacramentally and mystically, and he will come again in power and glory at the End Times. In the meantime, pray this Christmas season that the Lord will help those who doubt to find faith, those who despair to find hope, those who are weak to find courage, those who are sick to find health, those who are sad to find joy, and those who have died to find eternal life in God. And my prayer for you this Christmas:

> What better season for wrongs to be righted; for friends reunited; for new dreams to start ...
> What better season for mending and healing, for saying and feeling what's in the heart.
> What better season for love to keep glowing, for hope to start growing, for troubles to cease.
> What better season for sharing and giving, for once again living in joy and in peace!

Holy Family

Today we celebrate the feast of the holy family of Jesus, Mary, and Joseph. Before reflecting on the holy family, I heard a story over the holiday about a woman who died and suddenly found herself at the pearly gates of heaven. While she was waiting for Saint Peter, she peeked through the gates and saw handsome mansions and beautiful people she knew.

And when Saint Peter came by, the woman said, "This is such a breathtaking place! How do I get in?" Saint Peter told her, "You simply have to spell a word correctly." "And what's the word?" "Love." The woman correctly spelled "L-O-V-E," and Saint Peter welcomed her.

About a year later, this woman was walking by the gates, and Saint Peter asked her to guard the gates while he rushed up to see Jesus. She said, "No problem."

While she was guarding the gates, her husband suddenly arrived. And she said, "I'm surprised to see you so soon. What have you been doing since I died last year?"

The husband told her, "Oh, I've been doing very well since you died … In fact, I married the gorgeous young nurse who took care of you while you were ill. And then I won the lottery. I sold the little house you and I lived in for fifty years and bought a huge mansion overlooking the ocean. And my new wife—your nurse—she and I began traveling all around the world. In fact, today we were on vacation in Cancun, and I went water skiing. And I lost control of the ropes, hit my head against a rock, and here I am. What a bummer. How do I get in?"

"You have to spell a word correctly," his first wife told him.

"And so what's the word?" he asked.

"Czechoslovakia!"

He wasn't a good speller.

The word of God proclaimed is all about family. In the book of Genesis, Abraham worried that he was childless. But he puts his trust in God, and Abraham's wife had a son in their old age.

The author of Genesis challenged us to trust always in God, no matter how anxious we may be about a particular situation. God is near us, so our faith assures us, even if we don't think so.

Paul's letter to the Christian community in Colossae in western Turkey begins with the familial address: "Brothers and sisters." The author then spoke about qualities we should embody as family, qualities such as compassion, kindness, humility, gentleness, patience, forgiveness, and—above all—love.

Luke's Gospel tells us that when Mary and Joseph brought Jesus to the temple in Jerusalem, Simeon took Jesus in his arms and blessed God. Then Simeon praised God and said, "My eyes have seen your salvation ... a light." (Luke 2:30-32)

Then, home in Nazareth, Jesus grew strong and wise, and God's favor was upon him. His family was a vital factor while he was growing up.

More than two millennia later, Pope Francis placed the Synod on the Family under the care of the Virgin Mary and Saint Joseph. The pope saw this conference on family as a journey, with presentations imbued with faith, pastoral care, wisdom, and courage. And he described in his address a church that must have its doors wide open, especially to welcome the needy and the penitent. The Holy Father concluded, "Brothers and sisters, now we have one year to discern and find concrete solutions to so many challenges that families face today." In the meantime, Pope Francis invites families to spend time together, to listen and support one another, to share experiences, and to affirm the goodness in one another.

I think of the reflection titled "Children Learn What They Live." If children live with tolerance, they learn to be patient. If children live with encouragement, they learn confidence. If children live with praise, they learn to appreciate. If children live with fairness, they learn justice. If children live with security, they learn to have faith. If children live with approval, they learn to like themselves. If children live with acceptance and friendship, they learn to find love in the world. There's a thought-provoking reflection about all our relationships.

Pope Francis, among other things, urges families to develop a healthy sense of leisure. Yes, set aside time to do things together, to communicate. Sundays should be for family. Care for nature. As a family, talk about recycling, energy use, and so forth. Think positively about ourselves and other people. Live a life with as few regrets as possible. Someone wrote: "Twenty years from now we will be more disappointed by the things we didn't do than by the ones we did." Think about it.

Some may remember the popular 1970s and 1980s lecturer Leo Buscaglia, who authored such books as *Living, Loving and Learning* and *Born for Love*. One of his students wrote an article with a compelling message titled "Things You Didn't Do," describing the many times he erred and thought his father would yell at him, but his father didn't. The article ends like this: "There were lots of things you didn't do. You put up with me and you loved me. There were lots of things I wanted to thank you for when you returned from Vietnam. But you never did return!!!"

There's a compelling message: don't live a life of regrets. Our everyday lives aren't a dress rehearsal; they're the "real thing"; and to the extent that our lives are in our own hands, we should do good now, not later. Some of you may remember the Shakespearean actor John Barrymore, who electrified audiences with his portrayals of Hamlet and Richard III. Barrymore wrote that "a man [and a woman] is not old until regrets take the place of dreams."

Yes, that line is a wake-up call to us to live lives of no regrets. We should use our time, talents, and treasures for the good of others now, not later. Jesus, Mary, and Joseph lived lives together as a family, a holy family—lives with no regrets.

May God on this feast of the holy family grace us with faith in God as he graced Abraham and Sarah with the virtues in Paul's letter to the Colossians. And may God grace us, as he did Simeon and Anna, with the eyes of faith to see Jesus as our salvation, the Light who illuminates our darkness.

Epiphany

How many have read predictions for the New Year? If you find predictions bothersome, here's one consolation: more often than not, these forecasters have been wrong.

The Marquis de Condorcet, a French mathematician and philosopher, predicted in 1783 that there would be fewer revolutions. He found out how dead wrong he was ten years later when he died in a prison cell during the French Reign of Terror. Consider these other examples.

Water well drillers questioned an entrepreneur in 1859 about drilling for oil. "Drilling to find oil? You're crazy."

Thomas Watson, chairman of IBM, announced in 1943, "I think there is a world market for maybe five computers."

Ken Olson, founder of Digital Equipment, pronounced in 1977, "There is no reason anyone would want a computer at home."

The Wizard of Oz premiered in 1939 at theaters around the country. The original run time was predicted to be too long, so a song was cut at some previews. That song was "Somewhere over the Rainbow." Fortunately, after debates, MGM left the song in.

So much for predictions. Perhaps we might want to remember this prayer in the New Year: "God, grant me the serenity to accept the things I cannot change, courage to change the things I can, and the wisdom to know the difference."

Today we celebrate the Epiphany, the showing forth of the child Jesus to the magi. We really don't know whether they were wise men, astrologers, or spice traders. All we know is that they were non-Jews who had come from far away, guided by a mysterious star, a sudden illumination of wisdom, to pay homage to this Jewish child named Jesus. Yes, Jesus is for all people.

The word of God from Isaiah takes us back to the sixth century before Jesus, when the Jews lost everything they thought would continue forever: Jerusalem, the temple, and the monarchy. And despite this catastrophe, the author spoke of a New Jerusalem. A divine light will emanate from this Jerusalem, and all people, Jews as well as non-Jews, will acknowledge and walk by this light.

Christians, of course, see Jesus as this Light who illumines darkness, the Light who shows human beings the ultimate purpose of life. We are born to manifest the glory or presence of God through our time, talents, and treasures.

The letter of Paul to the Christian community at Ephesus in Turkey speaks about our future: we are coheirs to God's promise of eternal life, coworkers in bringing about the kingdom of God, and brothers and sisters to one another.

In the Gospel according to Matthew, we have all the ingredients of a great mystery novel: exotic visitors, a wicked king, court intrigue, a mysterious star, precious gifts, and a new child. The word of God became flesh so God could transform our earthly existence into an indescribable, heavenly one.

And the magi gave homage to this Christ child with gifts of gold, frankincense, and myrrh. Gold can symbolize royalty, kingship, or divinity, the things of God (and the coins of this Child's heavenly realm are compassion, forgiveness, and peace). Frankincense with its wonderful fragrance and medicinal magic can symbolize healing (and this Child came to heal our wounds and bridge the chasms that separate us from one another and from God). Myrrh or ointment can symbolize a burial embalmment (and this Child through his death or resurrection made us coheirs to God's promise of eternal life).

Now who is this child to whom the magi gave their homage? Who is this Jesus to whom we give our ultimate allegiance as a community of faith? The early Christian community saw Jesus as the fulfillment of the hopes of ancient Israel. And so they named him the Messiah, the anointed one. The more they reflected on who he was, the more they saw

Jesus not only as the fulfillment of their hopes but also the foundation of their hopes. And so they named him the eternal Word. The Gospel according to John captures this truth magnificently in the prologue: "In the beginning was the Word." Yes, Jesus was the foundation and fulfillment of all their hopes and our own.

This Jesus was a real historical person, flesh and blood like us. He experienced, as we do, fatigue, hunger, satisfaction, joy, friendship, disappointment, and loneliness. He was a rabbi, a teacher, and a prophet preaching that the kingdom of God was breaking into our midst. And Jesus worked signs and wonders that proclaimed that good ultimately would triumph over evil. He possessed authority to forgive wrongdoings, and he promised eternal life.

He had a unique relationship with the God of ancient Israel; he was one with God, but he was crucified and then rose from the dead. He is alive in our midst today, especially in the sacramental life of the Christian community. He is alive wherever two or three are gathered in his name, as we are gathered; and we too are alive with his grace and favor.

Jesus taught not only that the kingdom of God was breaking into our midst but also that you and I can share in this kingdom of God by living out a life of discipleship. And how is that? By living prayerfully in the presence of God; by recognizing that our lives do have an ultimate purpose; by seeing in Jesus, the Word made flesh, the face of God; by reaching out compassionately with a helping hand to the people around us; by experiencing the presence of the living Christ, body and blood, soul and divinity, sacramentally and mystically in this liturgy; and by always being ready to let go of our earthly lives in the mystery of death so that we can be one with God forever. Yes, in death is the hope of eternal life.

And Jesus taught that God is our Father, a compassionate God, always near us at the start of each day to guide us on our journey to our heavenly home.

So on this, the feast of the Epiphany or manifestation or showing forth of the glory or presence of God, I invite all of us to rededicate ourselves to Jesus Christ and to ask him to grace us anew at the beginning of this New Year so we might manifest ever more deeply the glory of God in our own lives.

I conclude with a New Year message a colonel friend of mine, doing humanitarian work in the Middle East, e-mailed me. We've not found the source, but these are great lessons:

The most destructive habit .... Worry
The greatest joy.. Giving
The greatest loss... Loss of self-respect
The most satisfying work .... Helping others
The ugliest personality trait .... Selfishness
The most endangered species............................. Dedicated leaders
Our greatest natural resource............................. Our young people
The greatest "shot in the arm"............................ Encouragement
The greatest problem to overcome....................... Fear
The most effective sleeping pill........................... Peace of mind
The most crippling failure disease....................... Excuses
The most powerful force in life .... Love
The most dangerous pariah.................................. A gossiper
The world's most incredible computer................. The brain
The worst thing to be without .... Hope
The deadliest weapon .... The tongue
The two most power-filled words......................... "I can."
The greatest asset .... Faith
The most worthless emotion................................ Self-pity
The most beautiful attire .... A smile
The most prized possession .... Integrity
The most powerful channel of communication ... Prayer
The most contagious spirit................................... Enthusiasm

This is truly something to live by: manifesting the glory or presence of God in our everyday attitudes and behaviors.

Baptism of the Lord

The image of water reminded me, for a moment, of a fire-and-brimstone preacher who railed against the evils of drink. He bellowed, "If I had all the beer in the world, I'd pour it into the river." Then he shouted, "And if I had all the wine in the world, I'd pour it into the river." And finally, he thundered, "And if I had all the whiskey in the world, I'd pour all the whiskey into the river."

As the preacher sat down, the song leader burst out, singing "Shall We Gather at the River." Yes, from the sermon humor circuit.

I don't know about you, but I notice more and more people with tattoos: colorful geometric designs, flowers and images, crosses, and so forth. Tattoos and brands are generally chosen as mark of identity. And anyone thinking about getting a tattoo should really want the tattoo, because getting rid of one can be painful.

Indelibility, identity—these are key aspects of what it means to be marked or tattooed. In baptism we have been branded, so to speak, and identified by God as belonging to a community of disciples. Yet baptism isn't a simple tattoo, rite, or milestone: it is a transformative experience, in which God lives in us and we live in God. That's our indelible identity. God's grace, God's favor, empowers us to live as disciples of Jesus.

Today we celebrate the baptism of Jesus by John in the Jordan River. And in this celebratory event, our Catholic community invites all of us to renew our own baptismal promises so we can live ever more transparently as disciples of Jesus, trying to do, as best we can, what is right and true and good.

The word of God, just proclaimed, takes us back in our imaginations to the sixth century before Jesus to the Hebrew exile in ancient Babylonia (what we know today as Iraq). The passage is a poem, a song, about the vocation or calling of a future "servant" who will be a Light to those who live in darkness, a doer of justice, a liberator to those who are addicted to vice, and a faithful keeper of God's covenant. The early Christian community saw this Hebrew "servant" Jesus, whose vocation or calling was to proclaim a transcendent purpose for us: eternal life with God beyond earthly life.

And this challenges us today to ask whether we are indeed a community of disciples, always trying as best we can to do what is right and true and good so we can reveal the glory or presence of God in our daily lives.

In the book of Acts of the Apostles, which is really the story about the beginnings of Christianity, the author described Peter, fired up by the grace of God, proclaiming Jesus as God's anointed One, the Messiah. You and I should be fired up by the grace of God and witnessing to Jesus by trying, as best we can, to live a life of virtue, one of self-discipline, compassion, responsibility, courage, friendship, honesty, loyalty, and faith in God.

In the Gospel according to Mark, John baptized Jesus in the waters of the Jordan River. As Jesus came up out of the waters, the power of God overwhelmed him, and Jesus, all fired up, began his public ministry in Galilee, proclaiming a new purpose for us, symbolized in a dove that suggests a new beginning or new creation after the flood in the Noah story.

Now John the Baptist is an interesting personality in the Gospels. He dressed simply and ate locusts and wild honey. But what was his vocation or calling? It was to point to Jesus as the Messiah. As we reflect on John's vocation, we might ask whether, by virtue of who we are and what we do, we reflect Jesus Christ in our relationships with one another. And what was John doing? He was baptizing. He was inviting people to turn their lives around, to turn toward God and away from selfishness.

Baptism is a rite of initiation into a community of disciples. In early Christianity, candidates were, more often than not, immersed in water. Water symbolizes life and death. It can be life giving (when we're dehydrated) or death threatening (Hurricane Sandy). When the candidate stepped into the pool and came up on the other side, he or she symbolized in that gesture a dying to selfishness and a rising to new life in God. By the eleventh century, baptism by immersion became the exception, and baptism by the pouring of water over the head of the candidate became the common practice.

Why be baptized? To understand baptism, we first need to understand who we are in a relationship with God. The book of Genesis captures this very graphically. In the beginning, Genesis says, man and woman walked with God; they had friendship with God and with one another. But somehow they lost that friendship. Genesis describes their fall very simply yet powerfully. They hid from God, man blamed woman, and even the earthly elements began to work against them. Ever since, the human family has cried out for God's friendship.

That is why God became flesh in Jesus of Nazareth. God, through Christ and empowered by the Spirit, reestablished that friendship. Thus baptism initiates us into a community of disciples of Jesus Christ, a fellowship of grace.

This new relationship with God makes very straightforward demands on us, summed up simply in the so-called Ten Commandments. The commandments are really ten statements about freedom from those attitudes and behaviors that undermine our relationship with God and one another.

The Ten Commandments say very simply that our God is a God of love, and our response to God's love is gratitude. This planet of ours and the people on it reflect the image of our God. And so everything on this planet—God's people especially—is worthy of reverence.

Yes, God deserves our time, and that's why we take time to get in touch with him. This same God challenges us to support virtues in our families—for example, caring for aging parents, cherishing life from beginning to end, being faithful with our marriage promises, respecting the rights of our siblings and others, speaking the truth, not exploiting people or treating them as objects, and being generous rather than greedy with what we have. The Ten Commandments underscore virtues we should practice every day.

Today, as we reflect on the baptism of Jesus, I invite us to renew our own baptismal promises, to live as sons or daughters of God, and to be a living gospel to others in this year of faith. Clinical psychologist Paul Gilbert put it this way: "You are writing a Gospel, A chapter each day, By deeds that you do, By words that you say." Pray for the grace to write your own living gospel so that others will recognize in you the glory or presence of God.

Jesus is the cornerstone, our light; and the apostles are the foundation of this community. And so today we ought to give thanks to God for the faith community to which we belong, a community that calls us to a life with God here and to eternal life beyond our earthly lives. We should take great pride in belonging to this worldwide Catholic community.

Second Sunday in Ordinary Time

Did you notice anything different in church today? The Christmas crèche is back in storage, and the poinsettias are gone. We are now in what we call "ordinary time." We are also in what we folks from the north call "winter."

You may have seen a story on the Internet –in various iterations -- about a couple who decided to go to Florida for a long weekend to escape an unusually cold winter in Minnesota. Both had jobs and couldn't coordinate their schedules to fly together. So the husband flew down first, checked into their favorite beach hotel, and found a newly installed computer in the hotel room. He decided to e-mail his wife back in Minnesota. But he left out one letter in her e-mail address, and the e-mail accidentally went to a widow in Texas who had just returned from her husband's funeral.

The widow was checking her e-mail, expecting messages of condolence from relatives and friends. But she fainted after reading the Minnesota man's message.

> To: My Loving Wife
> Subject: I've Arrived.
>
> I know you're surprised to hear from me, but they now have computers down here. I just checked in. Everything is ready for your arrival tomorrow. Looking forward to

seeing you and hoping your trip is as uneventful as mine.

PS. It sure is hot down here.

So much for high-tech messaging.

The word of God just proclaimed takes us back to the eleventh century before Jesus (the 1000s) to Israel, to a young man by the name of Samuel who slept close to the ark of the covenant.

Samuel heard a voice he eventually recognized as the voice of God, and he responded, "Speak, my God, for I am listening." And because he listened, Samuel went on to become one of the great prophets of Israel, anointer of kings and mouthpiece of God.

God speaks to us in many different ways just as he spoke to Samuel. The question is, are we listening? Since we got up this morning, God has been trying to speak to us through the beauty of nature; through the love of family, friends, and colleagues; and through the hymns we sing and the scripture we hear. In 101 different ways, God's voice is loud and clear. Unfortunately, we don't always hear God's voice because we're not always on the same wavelength; we're not on the right frequency.

Let me illustrate with a story shared by Rebecca Fine of The Science of Getting Rich Network. A young man was desperately seeking employment. He saw a "Help Wanted" ad for a telegraph operator. This fellow had no experience, but he did learn Morse code on his own, and he went to the telegraph office for an interview.

When he saw many other applicants, he became disheartened. But he sat down to wait for his turn. After only a few minutes, his face suddenly lit up. He stood up and went directly into the manager's office.

Within a few minutes, the manager appeared at the door with the young fellow and announced that he was hiring him for the telegraph job. The other applicants were astonished. One who had been waiting sputtered, "This isn't fair! We were here first but we never even got a chance, and he gets the job just like that?"

The manager answered, "All this time you were sitting here, the telegraph has been clicking away, saying: 'If you can understand this, come on into the office right now. You've got the job.' This young fellow was the only one of you who heard or understood the message."

Yes, God speaks to us in many different ways. But are we listening?

Are we on the same wavelength? Are we on the right frequency? Prayer—tuning in to the presence of God—puts us on the right frequency.

In his letter to the Christian community at Corinth, Paul spoke about our ultimate purpose: eternal life with God.

Yes, Paul said, we are living temples of God; God dwells within us, initially by virtue of baptism. We possess the spark of the divine, so to speak, within us. So, do we reflect the presence of God in our everyday attitudes and behaviors?

In today's Gospel according to John, we encounter John the Baptist and the disciples of Jesus. John pointed not to himself but to Jesus, the Lamb of God who takes away the sin of the world (the lamb, of course, refers to the Hebrew Passover or liberation from Ancient Egypt). Yes, the Lamb of God has freed us from death.

And then the Gospel speaks about the call of the disciples. Here we have the beginnings of a community of disciples, the church, what we know today as the worldwide Catholic faith community.

What kind of disciples are we? Are we grateful to belong to a worldwide Catholic faith community that stretches back almost two thousand years? Yes, there are many good reasons to be grateful disciples of Jesus in this worldwide Catholic faith community. Let me give you a few:

1. We are a worldwide community of believers that remembers Jesus (1.2 billion plus people: rich and poor, black and white, American, European, Asian and African), a family that celebrates the presence of the living Christ sacramentally and mystically in the liturgy.

2. We are a community with splendid heroes and heroines. We are the Church of Francis and Clare of Assisi, Dominic, Ignatius of Loyola, Teresa of Avila, Vincent de Paul, Therese of Lisieux, Popes John XXIII and John Paul II—and the litany of heroes and heroines goes on and on. These are people worth imitating in our own quest for a meaningful life.

3. We are a community that always has something to celebrate: the blessing of animals in October, the communion of saints in

November, Christmas, Ash Wednesday, Easter, Pentecost, the great feasts of the Virgin Mary—the list seems infinite.

4. We are also a community that takes a stand on peace and justice. The Catholic community sponsors and staffs shelters for the homeless and for battered women's safety, hospices for the terminally ill, soup kitchens, AIDS treatment centers, literacy programs, day care centers, hospitals, and schools throughout the world. And hundreds of Catholic relief and refugee agencies attempt to meet the basic needs of the poor.

Today the author of the book of Samuel speaks about a servant who listened to the voice of God. The author may ask us, "Do we pray regularly. Do we tune into the presence of God every day so that we can listen to God's voice?"

Paul may have asked us whether our attitudes and behaviors clearly reflect that we are living temples of God.

The author of the Gospel according to John may have asked us whether we, by the manner in which we live, point to Jesus as our way, truth, and life. And then the author of John described the beginnings of the church, the call of the disciples of Jesus.

Yes, Jesus is the foundation of our worldwide faith community. And we ought to give thanks to God for this community to which we belong, a community that calls us to a life with God here and now, and to eternal life.

Third Sunday in Ordinary Time

Remember those old radio and TV bloopers on YouTube? Church bulletin bloopers are also compiled on the Internet. One read, "Ladies, don't forget the rummage sale. It's a chance to get rid of those things not worth keeping around the house. Bring your husbands." Another said, "For those of you who have children and don't know it, we have a nursery downstairs." And finally, "Kevin Smith and Mary DiMarco were married last Saturday in the church. So ends a friendship that began in their high school days." The point is, proofread carefully.

How many have seen the film *Titanic* with Leonardo DiCaprio and Kate Winslet? James Cameron directed that film. He and his team descended three miles below the surface of the icy waters of the North Atlantic to see with their own eyes and photograph with their cameras evidence of history's greatest shipwreck.

But what really did sink this forty-five-thousand-ton floating hotel with first-class appointments, twenty-nine boilers in the engine room, and three anchors that weighed fifteen tons apiece? An update about an artifact posits that what really sank this forty-five-thousand-ton ship after it sideswiped an iceberg on the night of April 14, 1912, was a three-ounce key.

The ship had a crow's nest, a lookout, from which the crew could watch for icebergs. And in this crow's nest was a case or box containing a pair of high-powered binoculars, but this particular case had a secure lock. And unfortunately, when the *Titanic* went to sea with its twenty-two-hundred-plus passengers and crew, there had been a crew change, and someone in Southampton, England, forgot to leave the key with the lookout. As a result, they couldn't use the binoculars.

A ship that cost millions of dollars sinking because of something that cost only a few cents. And why? If the lookouts had possessed the key to the case, a surviving lookout testified they could have seen the iceberg with their binoculars and avoided sideswiping it.

What does a key to a case with binoculars have to do with the word just proclaimed? The binoculars can be understood, in one sense, as the eyes of our faith, through which we can see what lies beneath and beyond immediate appearances. In other words, this is the awesome reality of God in our lives.

The word of God first carries us back in the Hebrew scriptures to a man named Jonah. Whenever you hear the name Jonah, what do you think of? Three days in the belly of a whale or a character who brings bad luck wherever he goes? Actually the book of Jonah is a short story, about thirteen hundred English words. It's fiction (the Bible has many literary genres); yes, it's fiction with a simple message: God embraces everyone, Jew as well as Gentile. God asks only that we repent, that we orient our lives to God.

In the story God ordered Jonah to go to Nineveh, capital of Assyria (what we know today as modern Iraq) to preach repentance to the Ninevites. Jonah, of course, was shocked. The Ninevites weren't Jews; they were Gentiles. And so Jonah jumped into a boat and fled from God as far as he could. But eventually God caught up with Jonah, who preached God's repentance to the Ninevites. And the Ninevites shocked Jonah. They actually repented and oriented their lives toward God. With new eyes of faith, they recognized the awesome presence of God in their lives, and God spared the city of Nineveh. We may ask ourselves, "Do we recognize the presence of God in our lives?"

In his letter to the Christian community at Corinth in Greece, Paul challenged us to focus on the things of God, for the things of this world are passing away. We can focus so much on accumulating wealth and prestige and titles that we forget how transitory our lives really are. But with the eyes of faith, we believe that in the mystery of death we will pass, like Jesus before us, from this earthly life into a new, indescribable, transformative, heavenly reality. Paul may have been asking us, "Do we focus on the things of God?" And in the Gospel according to Mark, the disciples followed Jesus with the eyes of faith. They saw in him more than appearances.

But let's go back to the binoculars. If someone hadn't forgotten to give the key to the lookout in Southampton, England, perhaps the lookout would have seen the iceberg in the distance and alerted the captain to steer the *Titanic* away from harm. I like to think that the binoculars can be described as the eyes of faith, through which we can see what lies beneath and beyond immediate appearances. In other words, it is the reality of God in our lives.

Our faith, a gift from God, empowers us to relate to God. This faith attempts to answer the fundamental questions of human life, such as the following: Who am I? What am I living for? Where is my life going? Does anyone really care about what happens to me? What ultimately matters in life? And the content of our faith is expressed in belief statements such as the fourth-century Nicene Creed, which we profess in our liturgy.

We say, "I believe in one God," despite many folks today who experience not the presence, but the absence of God; despite the many who question the existence of God in the face of such overwhelming evils as disease, senseless violence, war and hunger.

Yes, we say, our God is "almighty, maker of heaven and earth," of all visible and invisible. We profess that there is someone completely other and completely beyond ourselves, One who is the cause and is responsible for everything that is: God, Father Almighty.

And yes, we believe in "one Lord, Jesus Christ." This Lord, Jesus Christ, for us and for our salvation "came down from heaven." Today there is so much brokenness on this planet; something is not quite right with this planet. There are hate, lies, injustice, greed, the denial of human rights, ignorance, and violence. This planet cries out for a healer, a reconciler. And this Jesus, who for our sake was crucified, died, was buried, and rose again, is our healer, our reconciler, our pledge of a life beyond this earthly life.

And yes, we believe in "the Holy Spirit, the Lord, the giver of life." The power of the Spirit is within us. And he enables us to take charge of our destiny and do good for others.

And we believe in "one, holy, catholic and apostolic community."

We "acknowledge one baptism" and "look toward the resurrection and the life to come."

This Nicene Creed underscores the essential content of faith; what we believe truly matters. May faith be the binoculars through which we see what lies beneath and beyond immediate appearances; that is, the reality or presence of God all around us, within us, and in one another.

Fourth Sunday in Ordinary Time

There's a maritime legend – perhaps meant as humor but pointing to a truth -- about a ship captain at sea in the midst of fog. He saw what looked like the lights of another ship heading toward him. He had his signalman blink, "Change your course ten degrees south."

A reply came back: "Change your course ten degrees north."

The captain of the ship answered, "I'm a captain. Change your course south."

To which the reply was, "I am a seaman, first class. Change your course north."

This infuriated the captain, so he signaled, "Change your course south. I'm on a battleship!"

To which the reply came back: "I'm a lighthouse. Your call."

As we journey sometimes in a sea of darkness, wondering if we're going in the right direction, let Jesus be our lighthouse, so to speak.

The word of God today carries us back over three thousand years to the thirteenth century before Jesus (the 1200s) to Moses, a prophet or mouthpiece of God who spoke to the Hebrews "in peals of thunder and hail." (Exodus 9:23) Such experiences terrified the Hebrews. And so Moses promised them future prophets, mouthpieces of God, who would be the voice of God throughout triumphs and tragedies. These prophets would have the courage to speak truth and justice, freedom and peace, despite the cost to themselves.

The early Christian community saw in this prophecy Jesus as the End Times prophet, the definitive mouthpiece of God, our way, our truth, and our life. Paul urged the Christian community in Corinth in Greece not to be anxious about their lives but to live a God-centered life every day, because the End Times are near. And in the Gospel according to Mark, Jesus entered a synagogue and amazed his listeners with his compelling words and awesome power. Even the demons recognized Jesus as the holy one of God. And here Jesus exorcized a "crazed" man.

Mark's Gospel highlights the struggle between the kingdom of God and the kingdom of Satan. In fact, Satan is cited thirty-four times in the New Testament. He is "the tempter," "the evil one," "the enemy," "the adversary," and "the prince of devils." And Jesus was forever driving these "devils" or "demons" out of people.

Yes, the kingdom of God will triumph over the kingdom of Satan, and good ultimately will conquer evil. But how can we understand evil? How do we understand evil in the form of suffering?

For the Christian, the problem of evil can be best understood in light of the mystery of the dying and rising of Jesus. Yes, our Christian faith proclaims that hidden in every Good Friday is an Easter hope or joy. Think about it.

Someone in a family, for example, loses a job, is diagnosed with a life-threatening illness, sees a relationship begin to unravel, or has to care for a seriously ill parent or child. And then this family draws together, supports one another, and gradually brings faith, hope, and love to their life together as a family.

Yes, the faith, hope, and love of a family can transform a tragic Good Friday, so to speak, into an Easter hope. We sometimes find ourselves stuck in a Good Friday situation—our problems sometimes may seem to overwhelm us. Our faith challenges us to remember that good will ultimately conquer evil, that love transforms hate, and that light shatters the darkness.

The life of Jesus didn't end in the tragedy of the cross but in the triumph of the resurrection. Hidden within the mystery of suffering is the glory of resurrection, eternal life, a transfigured and indescribable new life.

As I reflect on evil in light of Mark's Gospel, I think of a story by Elie Wiesel, the Nobel Prize winner and survivor of concentration camps. In one of Wiesel's works, *Night*, he described how the SS guards marched all the inmates to the parade grounds and there hanged a youngster—all because an inmate had escaped and as a warning to the other inmates. As the youngster hung there, dying, Wiesel, a youngster himself, heard a voice behind him say, "Where is God now?"

This is an eternal question, highlighted in the biblical book of Job, in *The Confessions of St. Augustine*, in the literature of Fyodor Dostoevsky, and in best sellers like Rabbi Harold Kushner's *When Bad Things Happen to Good People*.

Yes, as we reflect on the human situation today, brutal violence by ISIS in the Middle East, the denial of basic human rights in some countries, and systemic poverty in so many regions of the globe, we realize that the entire planet cries out for God's grace, God's healing power.

There is, of course, no satisfactory answer to the mystery of evil. At times suffering does result from immoral behavior, from the misuse of freedom. Think, for example, of the tyrants of the twentieth century: Adolph Hitler, Joseph Stalin, Mao Tse-tung, and Pol Pot in Cambodia. These tyrants and so many others misused their freedom and caused untold suffering. They personified evil.

At other times, suffering, for example, results from natural disasters like earthquakes, typhoons, and tornadoes; from an unfinished, incomplete universe, a universe on the way; and from a universe in process toward an ultimate goal.

But ultimately, suffering is a mystery. So how can we respond to it?

We have to remember that God is always near us. He forever seeks to bring us to a fuller life. God will never abandon us. Chisel in your memories the words of the prophet Isaiah: "Can a woman forget her infant…Even should she forget, I will never forget you." (Isaiah 49:15)

Second, if we suffer, we should avoid negative judgments about ourselves. To say "I really deserve it" is a form of self-hate. And finally, remember the mystery of suffering has healing and redemptive power.

Yes, our everyday inescapable suffering, borne with love, can be redemptive; it can bring forth goodness and new life in us and in others. We can say this because the sufferings of Jesus brought forth eternal life, resurrection for all.

The ultimate, of course, is death. How do we come to terms with our own dying? Most of us don't long with Saint Paul to be free from this earthly life so that we can be with the Risen Jesus. Many pass through Elisabeth Kübler-Ross's stages of death and dying: denial, anger, bargaining, depression, and ultimately acceptance.

There is a darkness about death that even Jesus cried out against. Death seems cruel; it destroys, and yet in the Christian vision, we expect that the Spirit, who continually amazes us, will surprise us in the moment of our own dying. We cannot begin to imagine what life after this earthly life will be like, but we know the Spirit will satisfy our deepest needs and longings. "What eye has not seen, and ear has not heard, and what has not entered the human heart, what God has prepared for those who love him." (1 Cor. 2:9)

And so, as we reflect on the mystery of evil in light of Mark's Gospel, let us remember that hidden in the sufferings of Jesus on Good Friday was the glory of his resurrection on Easter. And hidden within our own inescapable suffering is the glory of eternal life.

Fifth Sunday in Ordinary Time

The Super Bowl is history. How many remember the last seconds of the game? A single call makes all the difference between winning and losing.

We can easily interpret our own lives as a game. Right now, it's halftime, so to speak. What are we going to do differently to win the game of life—eternal life? Think about it.

The book of Job, just proclaimed, carries us back in our imaginations to the wisdom literature of ancient Israel. Biblical scholars describe this book as a poetic drama dealing with the problem of evil and yet offering no easy answers.

The Bible, of course, is made up of many literary genres: prose, poetry, drama, mythology, legend, parables, fiction, songs, oracles and history; and these biblical books have to be understood within the context of their literary genres. Moreover, the Old Testament text, as we know it, evolved over centuries.

The book of Job brings us face-to-face with the mystery of suffering and evil. As the legend begins, Job had everything he could possibly want: health, wealth, family, and friends. But gradually he lost everything he had and ended up a broken man on a dung heap, taunted by his friends.

Job asked, "How could this happen to me?" But the better question might have been not "How could this happen to me?" but "How will I respond to these misfortunes? How will I deal with them?"

Job's friends said he must have deserved them, but Job protested his innocence. And then God spoke to Job in a whirlwind. He didn't answer

Job's questions at all: Why do bad things happen to good people? Why evil? Why injustice? Hunger? Brutal violence? Natural disasters?

Job, in so many words, cried out, "I don't understand."

And God said, "That's right, Job, you don't."

God didn't answer the questions; he simply let Job experience God's awesome presence in some mystical way. In the final analysis, there is no satisfactory answer to the mystery of suffering and evil.

Nonetheless, our faith in Jesus—who is risen, alive, among us, and transformed into a new heavenly reality—proclaims loudly that suffering and death aren't the final reality; healing, new life, and resurrection are.

And in the meantime Jesus challenged us to fight against evil and suffering; and to heal, console, forgive, and create compassionate communities where people can experience responsible freedom, fairness, peace, truth, and opportunity.

In his letter to the Christian community at Corinth in Greece, Paul described his one passion in life, proclaiming the good news: Jesus was risen, alive, among us, and transformed into a new heavenly reality. His resurrection was the pledge of our own eternal life.

That's the truth that energized Paul. And the question for us is, what energizes us? What ignites us? Where do we find meaning or purpose? In our family? In our job? In our volunteer service? In our experiences, whether sports, friends, music, reading, or nature? Probably in all these.

And eventually we have to find meaning in the mystery of our own dying where we will have to let go of our own earthly life and make a leap of faith into the hands of God forever—much like a trapeze performer.

In the Gospel according to Mark, Jesus made a house call to Peter's mother-in-law. He healed her, and she immediately prepared dinner. The townspeople suddenly appeared at Peter's house with their sick ones. And Jesus continued to work signs and wonders, healings, and exorcisms that signaled the breaking in of the kingdom of God.

Imagine we were at Capernaum that day; what so-called demon, addiction, or character flaw (for example, greed, lying, prejudice, or hate) would we ask Jesus to drive out of us?

And then Jesus continued his purpose-driven life and proclaimed that human beings have a destiny beyond this earthly life: eternal life with God. Yes, that was the incredibly awesome vision of Jesus.

The risen Christ, by virtue of the waters of baptism, empowers us to choose our better selves, to give our time and talent to others, and to take a stand for what is true, fair, and right. That is what our baptismal calling is all about. Every one of us has gifts or talents that can empower or "build up" other people.

It often seems that our culture is celebrity driven, but celebrities such as Bradley Cooper in *American Sniper,* or Angelina Jolie, Oprah Winfrey, and Tom Brady aren't the only people who have gifts or talents. You and I have special gifts or talents by virtue of our baptism: we possess the power to believe, hope, and love.

And within Catholic and Christian life there are many splendid callings: father or mother, teacher or student, doctor or lawyer or businessperson. Whoever you are, you have a specific vocation, a calling, right now to empower people to choose their better selves, to give their time and talents to others, and to take a stand for what is true, good, and right by simply being examples of such a lifestyle ourselves. And what makes us faithful and effective Catholics and Christians is the Spirit of God within us.

Oh, personality can be a blessing; it's great if we easily warm up to people. But more importantly, the Spirit of God works through us as we are. He illumines our minds to know the way we should behave and strengthens us to behave in that way despite obstacles. He gives us his gifts: "love, joy, peace, patience, goodness, faithfulness, gentleness and self-control." (Gal. 5:22-23)

What more can we want? The Spirit of God alone can make us a means of healing, a channel of grace, or an instrument of peace. What a wonderful gift.

These gifts or talents we have aren't for ourselves but for others, for the common good, for the family in which we live, the profession in which we work, and the community in which we find ourselves. The gifts we have look beyond ourselves to our lives with others. No Christian is an island. The Spirit empowers us, as we are, to help others become more human, more godlike in their relationships with other people.

I close with a prayer for you that sums up some of these thoughts about meaning and purpose. I've shared it in homilies, not sure of the original source:

Fortunate are the persons,
Who in this life can find,
A purpose that can fill their days
And goals to fill their mind.
For in this world there is a need,
For those who'll lead the rest,
To rise above the "average" life,
By giving of their best!
Will you be one, who dares to try
When challenged by the task,
To rise to heights you've never seen,
Or is that too much to ask?

May we all realize that in the end the purpose of life is to matter, to make a difference for the better, by giving the best we have in service to one another.

Sixth Sunday in Ordinary Time

Valentine's Day brings back youthful memories for me. Like most students, I had very little money, but I decided to buy my "Valentine" a gift. I went into a gift shop and said to the saleswoman at the counter, "I'd like to buy a Valentine's gift. What do you have?" And so she took a gift off the shelf and placed it on the counter.

I said, "How much??"

The reply was, "That will be fifty dollars."

I said, "I would like to see something cheaper." She showed me another gift? I said, "How much?"

"That will be twenty-five dollars."

I said to her, "You don't understand. I'm a student with little money. I want to see something really cheap." And she handed me a mirror. The saleswoman was obviously from New York City, my hometown.

The word of God, just proclaimed, takes us back to one of the early books of the Bible: Leviticus, which was named after the tribe of Levi. It's a rule book. This book describes sacrificial religious rituals and rubrics, festivals, public health protocols, a holiness or "how-to-behave code" in our covenantal relationships with God and our fellow human beings.

The author gives his fellow Hebrews a guideline about so-called leprosy, which in those days referred not to what we know today as Hansen's disease but to skin diseases of one kind or another. These skin diseases were thought to be infectious or contagious, so a person, if declared "unclean," was banished from the community. He or she had to live outside the community, alone and isolated. The word of God here challenges us to reach out compassionately to the lonely, the sick, the needy, and the forgotten.

In his letter to the Christian community at Corinth, Paul was adjudicating a dispute about whether Christians could eat meat or other foods associated with temple rituals of ancient Rome. Paul said that yes, they could eat these foods but not to do so if it scandalized fellow Christians. Don't argue over what you may eat or drink, Paul said. "Whether you eat or drink, or whatever you do, do everything for the glory of God." (1 Cor. 10:31)

Paul challenged us to work for the good of others; to live out the virtues Jesus highlighted, for example, in the beatitudes and elsewhere in the Gospels; and to let our fellow human beings see in our attitudes and behaviors the "glory or presence of God."

In the Gospel according to Mark, a so-called leper begged Jesus to restore him to good health. This man wasn't supposed to be around people. He was isolated … unable to live with his family, hold a job, or attend services in the synagogue … He was rejected. And yet this man chose to face yet another rejection by walking up to Jesus. And Jesus, "moved with pity," healed him and went on to say, "Tell no one"—the so-called messianic secret. (Mark 1:41-44)

There's an old saying that the only secret is the one that's told to no one. But the point I want to highlight is this: the leper's prayer was answered. Yes, sometimes our prayers are answered, but more often they're not. We may pray to God for one thing or another and hear only silence. We're ill, or someone we love has cancer. We feel insecure about our job in this global economy. We become anxious about our children. We pray for peace and understanding in our families. We pray that a particular wrong will be righted and so forth. And God seems so silent. We may even feel like giving up on God, or we may start thinking negatively about ourselves. What to do?

Let us pray not to succumb to these negative feelings but to rise above them by reflecting on certain faith themes:

1. Let's reexamine our image of God. Some people think of God only as a judge. However, the Bible, which captures the religious

experiences of so many men and women, offers a collage of God images. God is a walking companion in Genesis, a passionate debater in the book of Job, an anxious parent, a comforting mother in the book of Isaiah, and a prodigal Father in the Gospels. Yes, what is our image of God? God is our ever-faithful companion in life.

2. Imagine what it would be like if all our prayers were answered. The ancient Greek storyteller Aesop told a story of a dog who found a bone and pranced happily homeward. Passing by a pond, he saw a dog that looked like himself with a similar bone. And lurching forward to steal the bone, the dog's own bone fell into the water—and he discovered the other dog had been only his reflection. Too much greed results in nothing. Bernie Madoff should have read this fable. My point is this: sometimes in our prayers, there's too much of us and not enough of God and our fellow human beings.

3. Remember God's providence and care for us in the past. How often the ancient Hebrews forgot the wonders God worked in Egypt, in the wilderness, in the kingdom of Israel. Like a skilled pickpocket, God is present in many different ways, and we don't know except by the evidence afterward. He may seem absent, but our faith says he's in our midst.

4. Be angry but don't stay angry. In his novel *The Town Beyond the Wall*, holocaust survivor Elie Wiesel described the anger of a concentration camp inmate who said, "I shake my fist at God; it's my way of saying God exists." That shout became a prayer. Prophets and saints often argued with God. Yes, to demand an answer is to take God seriously, to acknowledge God's care. But we ultimately have to let go of our anger; otherwise that anger will be poison. Remember the prayer: "God, grant me the serenity to accept the things I cannot change, courage to change the things I can, and the wisdom to know the difference."

5. Know you are in good company. Many others have known the silence of God, including Job in the Bible. Jesus prayed for deliverance. The point I want to make is this: keep praying, for God is God. God's ultimate purpose is to satisfy our deepest longings with eternal life.

So as we think about the leper whose prayer was answered and about our own prayers, remember God's care for us in the past and his continuing care for us.

The great sixteenth-century saint Teresa of Avila, declared a Doctor of the Church by Pope Paul VI, gives us this perspective, which I will quote:

> Let nothing disturb you;
> Let nothing dismay you;
> All things pass;
> God never changes;
> Patience gains everything;
> They who have God
> Lack nothing:
> God alone suffices.

First Sunday in Lent

I heard a story about three youngsters bragging about their fathers. The first boy said, "My dad scribbles a few words on a piece of paper, calls it a poem, and they give him one hundred dollars."

The second boy boasted, "That's nothing. My dad scribbles a few words on a piece of paper, calls it a song, and they give him one thousand dollars."

The third boy bragged, "I got you both beat. My dad scribbles a few words on a piece of paper, calls it a sermon, and it takes eight people to collect all the money!"

I also read about an elderly woman who recently died. She requested no male pallbearers. In her handwritten instructions for her memorial service, she wrote, "They wouldn't take me out while I was alive; I don't want them to take me out when I'm dead."

Last Wednesday, Ash Wednesday, we began our lenten journey to Easter. The word *Lent* comes from an Anglo-Saxon word that means "spring." And spring means life. The snow will melt, and the landscape will turn green again. Believe me, Bostonians long for that change.

Lent is a time to renew ourselves. It's time for a change of heart, a time to become more aware of God's presence in our daily lives, and a time to give closer attention to the needs of one another.

I begin with a true story about a father and son. The father could barely make ends meet; his wife was chronically sick. And life for the three of them was a succession of small apartments, simple meals, second- and third-hand furniture, and hand-me-down clothes.

All the son wanted was to escape this kind of life, and eventually he did. By age forty, he realized the American dream: he was partner with an investment firm, had a beautiful home and family, and possessed more than enough money to be comfortable.

And then his father died; his mother had died years before. After his father's death, the son went to his father's apartment, and in a closet, the son—who had thought his father died as a failure—found a box of memorabilia. He discovered a letter his father had written years before when the son was born. The letter began with his father's usual greeting: "Hi, Johnny."

> I'm your daddy. I've waited so long to say that. The doctors told your mom and me we could never have a child of our own. But every day we prayed for a miracle. And much to everyone's surprise, you were born: our miracle child. Johnny. To be your daddy means picking you up when you fall and holding you when you are afraid. There's so much in my heart, so many dreams for you. You have brought joy into our lives, a joy your mom and I thought we'd never know.
>
> Son, I'll never be rich. But I believe that when God helped us find our way to you, God would also be "beside us" the rest of our lives. We would always have each

other, and that's more than I ever hoped for. Just keep
in mind who you are, where you've come from, and how
much we love you, our miracle child.

It was only then that the son began to have a change of heart; he
realized the things that mattered the most: his family and the people
around him.

His greatest regret was that he hadn't been attentive enough to his
father. A challenge to all of us is to do the best we can every day so we
won't have a life of regrets.

The point, and the point of Lent, is this: So often people search for
meaning and purpose in such things as wealth, power, celebrity, and
leisure. And in the process they forget the things that truly matter: our
relationship with God and our relationships with one another, especially
with our families.

Lent challenges us to refocus ourselves on the things that truly
matter, to have a change of heart, to become more aware of God's
presence in our lives, and to pay closer attention to the needs of one
another.

The book of Genesis speaks about God's covenant with Noah and
the human family, summed up in the simple but splendid phrase "You
are my people; and I am your God." And the sign of the covenant is a
rainbow, inviting us to recognize the link between heaven and earth,
between God and ourselves, and to rededicate ourselves to our baptismal
promises.

In the letter of Peter, we see the history of our salvation through
the lens of Jesus's death and resurrection. Jesus reestablished a right
relationship between us and God, and the Spirit of God deepens that
relationship. And the image of Noah and the ark alludes to our baptism
and call to be faithful to our promises.

In the Gospel, Jesus was in the wilderness for forty days where he
overcame the dark or evil forces of human existence and then began
his public ministry of preaching that the kingdom of God was at hand.
"Repent and believe in the Gospel." (Mark 1:15)

My good friends, during this lenten season let us examine the course
or direction of our lives. Are we on the right track, so to speak? Do we

have our priorities straight? And if we're a bit off course, how can we get back on track?

That's why the church invites us focus on three disciplines to make sure we're on the right track: prayer, fasting, and almsgiving. The church urges us to treat ourselves to these age-old disciplines of our Christian/ Catholic community.

1. Yes, retreat ourselves to prayer. Prayer is an awareness of our absolute dependence on God, a grateful response to God for our very fragile lives. Prayer simply brings to consciousness the presence of God that is already around us and within us. Now there are many approaches to prayer: familiar prayers like the Our Father, this Eucharistic liturgy, and the prayer of silence or petition. All these approaches to prayer are simply windows or pathways into the presence of God. How often and how well do we pray? Even now, am I entering as fully as possible into this Eucharistic liturgy by participating wholeheartedly in the singing, listening as attentively as possible to the word of God proclaimed.

2. Second, retreat ourselves to fasting. Fasting is a gospel value but not fasting alone. Fasting and almsgiving are gospel twins. For the early Christians, going without food enabled the hungry to eat. But fasting is more than eating. Our lenten fast can mean doing without other things: anger, impatience, selfishness, negative judgments about others, or whatever really prevents us from living a life of discipleship with Jesus.

3. And finally retreat ourselves to almsgiving. In early Christianity there were no government agencies to provide assistance to the poor, the needy, the homeless, the underprivileged, and the sick. Therefore, almsgiving was seen as an essential addition to prayer and fasting not only during Lent but also every day. Share what we have with and for others. We should share our time—take time to visit, listen, and write. We should share our talents and money with needy people, if we can. We should share ourselves

and smile more often to let others know we want them to share your joy.

Yes, as we begin this lenten season, it's time for a change of heart. It's time to become more aware of God's presence in our lives through prayer and to pay closer attention to the needs of others.

And so I invite all of us to rediscover and retreat ourselves to prayer, fasting, and almsgiving so we can refocus on what truly matters: our relationships with God and our fellow human beings.

Second Sunday in Lent

I begin with a true story about a nurse in a hospital emergency room who escorted a young man to the bedside of a dying, elderly patient. She whispered a few times into the ear of this dying man, "Your son is here." The patient could barely see the young man; he simply reached out his hand, and the young man squeezed it. The young man sat, holding his hand. About a half hour later, the old man died.

The nurse began to offer her condolences. But then the young man asked, "Who was that man?"

The startled nurse said, "I thought he was your father."

"No, I never saw him before."

"But then why didn't you say something when I took you to him?"

The young man simply said, "In the waiting room, when you asked whether I was this dying man's son, I knew from the expression on your face and in your voice that this man needed his son right away. And when I realized he was too sick to tell whether or not I was his son, I knew how much he needed me."

Like the disciples in today's Gospel who suddenly saw Jesus with "the eyes of God," this young man saw a patient with the eyes of God. And in God's eyes, we are all brothers and sisters to one another, sons and daughters of God, our Father. This young man possessed a vision of God, a vision that enabled him to become a "son" to the dying man. And this Lent season invites us to refocus on the things of God, to see with the eyes of God one another as brothers and sisters, sons and daughters of God, our Father.

The word of God takes us back in our imaginations almost four thousand years to the ancient Near East, to Israel, and to a man by the name of Abraham, a model of complete trust in God, a faith-filled human being. Abraham's call was a watershed in the history of our salvation. Here God put Abraham to the test: "Take your son Isaac, your only one...offer him up...." (Gen. 22:2) Now we may wonder, *What kind of God would ask such a thing?* But Abraham had committed himself completely to God and responded unconditionally; he would do whatever God asked. And for his complete and total trust, God spared Isaac and assured Abraham of land, prosperity, and children.

That complete trust in God, in all the uncertainties and hazards of life, is a challenge to us as well, especially when things aren't going the way we want them to go or when the future seems so uncertain and hazardous.

In his letter to the Christian community in Rome, Paul invited them to be men and women of courage. "If God is for us, who can be against us?" (Rom. 8:31) God sent his only Son into our midst—the Word become flesh—and this Jesus, through his death and resurrection, reestablished our relationship with God. Paul urged us to persevere in our lives of discipleship with Jesus so we could be transformed, like the glorified Jesus before us, into a new heavenly creature.

In the Gospel according to Mark, the disciples experienced the transfiguration of Jesus; they saw the unique and awesome presence of God in Jesus of Nazareth. And as the scriptures describe, he was transfigured before them and his clothes "became dazzling white," an allusion to the white cloth given to us at baptism. (Mark 9:2-3) The disciples suddenly saw a vision of the "glorious" Jesus beyond the Jesus of flesh and blood in their everyday lives. They saw the face of God in Jesus. Our ultimate destiny is our own transfiguration into the image of the "glorious" Jesus. We are citizens of another realm, a heavenly realm, and to be a citizen is to be in a relationship with God here and now.

Our relationship with God challenges us to practice virtue. Someone summed up the practice of virtue as simply living the "Four Rs": responsibility, right, respect, and religion.

First is responsibility. Commit yourself to excellence in whatever you do.

Second is right. Do what's right. There are many examples of people who did the right thing despite the consequences: Mahatma Gandhi, Rosa Parks, Martin Luther King Jr., Nelson Mandela, and Oscar Romero. Their challenge was to make a difference for the better. How relevant are the words of the great eighteenth-century British statesman Edmund Burke: "The only thing necessary for evil to triumph is for good people to do nothing." And always remember the ten most powerful two-letter words: "If it is to be, it is up to me."

Third is respect. We should respect one another, even if we agree to disagree. We are all brothers and sisters to one another, sons and daughters of God, our Father. God lives in us, and we live in God. Each and every human person has been created in the image and likeness of the One who is the origin of all that is. Jesus challenged us to settle our differences, not by complaining to everyone else but by going directly to explore solutions. Conflicts are inevitable in human relationships, but if dealt with constructively, they can create even better, lifelong relationships. So all of us must be willing to forgive and forget so-called injuries and work together to create a family of God that reflects responsibility, right (doing what's right), respect, and religion.

And finally there is religion. The word *religion* derives from a Latin word *re-ligare*, which means "to tie together." How do we tie our lives together? How do we make sense of our lives? It's no accident that we're here. How do we weave the myriad experiences of life into a meaningful fabric? For example, all of us experience "awe."

We live around eighty or ninety years on a planet that is billions of years old. We experience beauty and love. We create life. We recognize astonishing courage, integrity, and compassion. Similarly, we witness appalling brutality, cruelty, greed, and injustice. We search for meaning in a welter of experiences; we seek connectedness to our fellow human beings. We recognize the frailty of our lives; we age and eventually die. This is the human predicament. We ask, is there a power beyond us who can help us make sense out of our lives?

The Christian answer is, of course. That awesome power is God, who became flesh in Jesus of Nazareth and is alive by the breath of the Spirit, who is the mystery of the triune God. This God calls us to be in a relationship and to reflect his presence and glory in our everyday lives and behavior. And that is religion. During the lenten season, we might reflect on these Four Rs and ask, how might the practice of these virtues deepen our relationship with God and each other?

Third Sunday in Lent

An elderly couple had dinner at another couple's house, and after eating, the wives went into the kitchen. Meanwhile, the two men were talking at the table, and one said, "Last night we went to a new restaurant, and I would recommend it very highly."

The other man said, "What is the name of the restaurant?"

The first man thought and thought, and finally said, "What is the name of that flower you give to someone you love? It's red with thorns."

"Do you mean the rose?"

"Yes, that's it," replied the man. He turned toward the kitchen and yelled, "Rose, what's the name of that restaurant we went to last night?"

So much for forgetting.

The word of God carries us back in our imaginations over three thousand years to the ancient Near East, to the Sinai Peninsula between Egypt and Israel, and to a charismatic leader named Moses.

At Sinai, God entered into a covenant with the Hebrews, summed up in that simple yet profound statement "You are my people and I am your God." Yes, God would keep his promises if the Hebrews kept theirs. In other words, they must live up to the demands of the covenant: recognize their absolute dependency on God, worship God alone, support their families, reverence human life, keep their marriage vows, respect the rights of other people, speak truthfully, be chaste, and replace greed with generosity.

These commandments are basic guidelines for good behavior. The question for you and me is, are these guidelines ours?

In his letter to the Christian community at Corinth, Paul spoke about how people look for signs of power or the wisdom of philosophers before they will believe in the mystery of the dying and rising of Jesus Christ. Paul here proclaimed that the mystery of the death and resurrection of Jesus Christ is indeed our power and wisdom. He challenged us to center our lives on the mystery of the dying and rising of Jesus Christ. Why? Because hidden in every Good Friday suffering is the glory of Easter.

In the Gospel according to John, Jesus cleansed the temple of buying and selling, predicted his death and resurrection, and proclaimed that the community of believers would replace the temple in Jerusalem. Yes, a new order would replace the old one. Jesus was indeed the new temple of God, the presence of God among us. Elsewhere Paul proclaimed that we ourselves are temples of God; the triune God lives within us by virtue of the waters of baptism.

During these lenten days, we continue to practice the age-old lenten disciplines of prayer, fasting, and almsgiving, In particular, I ask all of us to tune into the presence of God as we go about our daily routines.

We sometimes are like radios or TVs not tuned into a station or channel. The newscasters and entertainers are out there talking and singing away. The station is beaming live signals. But there's no communication between us and the station, and that often may be our problem with God. God is out there—and God is also deep within us—beaming forth his life and light and love, but we don't tune ourselves into the presence of God. We fail to pray.

What then is prayer? Whether we know it or not, we are already in the presence of God. Prayer simply brings to our consciousness God's presence, which is already around and within us.

There are many pathways, approaches, or guides to prayer. We simply have to find our own style of prayer. But I would like to explore ever so briefly some approaches to prayer that can enrich our own friendship with God.

Familiar prayers include the Our Father, the stations of the cross, the mysteries of the rosary, and the peace prayer of St. Francis. All these, when pondered slowly, can be pathways or passages into the presence of God. Yes, they can enrich our friendship with God. Above all, this liturgy, the most perfect prayer of the Christian community, is the primary pathway or approach into the presence of God.

Praise is another approach. Praise is the bubbling over of the Spirit of God within us. Francis of Assisi was forever singing praises. He saw the face of God in the sun and moon, wind and water, earth and flowers, and trees and people. Francis captured the praise of God in his magnificent "Canticle of the Sun," also known as "Canticle of the Creatures." He even included a passage praising God for our sister bodily death, from whose embrace no living person can escape. To praise God is to recognize that fundamental relationship between ourselves as creatures and God as our Creator and our ultimate destiny.

Another approach to prayer is to take a favorite passage of scripture and slowly meditate on the meaning of it. We each have favorite passages. Mine are "I am the Way, the Truth and the Life," "Come to me all you who find life burdensome, and I will refresh you," and "Whatever you do to the least of these, you do for me." What is your favorite passage? To slowly reflect on scripture can be a window into the presence of God.

Another approach to prayer is the Jesus Prayer, which in its fullest form is, "Lord Jesus Christ, Son of the living God, have mercy on me a sinner." It is similar to the prayer "Jesus, Son of David, have mercy on me." Some people link the Jesus Prayer with their breathing. They shorten the prayer to "Jesus, mercy," breathing in on "Jesus" and breathing out on "mercy." I'm not suggesting that you do this, but I'm saying that this can also bring you into the presence of God.

There are many other approaches to prayer. There is the prayer of silence. Without any thought, word, or image, we calmly feel the presence of God within us.

There is the prayer of petition. Like Jesus, in the garden of Gethsemane for example, we shouldn't hesitate to pray for our needs and those of others. The prayer of petition recognizes again that fundamental relationship between the Creator and the creature.

There is the prayer of suffering. Jesus is the model for this prayer. Afraid in the garden of Gethsemane and in pain on the cross, he trusted ever more deeply in the love of his Father. Yes, Jesus trusted that God would bring him out of the darkness of death into the light of the resurrection.

Almost anything we see or experience can be a pathway or passageway into the presence of God. All kinds of things we do in our day-to-day activities can make us aware of God's presence. Francis of Assisi saw all creatures as windows, passageways, or pathways into the presence of God.

And so during this lenten season, I pray that we will become more aware of God's presence around and within us. We are indeed living temples of God. And, in particular, I pray that this liturgy will be a window or passageway into the presence of God for all of us.

Fourth Sunday in Lent

Every now and then I stop at a bookstore to browse. One title caught my eyes: *Disorder in the American Courts*, which quotes transcripts of things people actually said in court. For example, one attorney asked, "Do you recall the time that you examined the body?"

The witness replied, "The autopsy started around eight p.m."

The attorney: "And Mr. Denton was dead at the time?"

The witness: "If not, he was by the time I finished."

In another case, an attorney asked a witness to describe an individual. The reply was, "Medium height and had a beard."

The attorney followed up. "Was this a male or a female?"

The witness answered, "Unless the circus was in town, I'm going with male."

The book makes for humorous reading about things people actually said in court.

Now what does the word of God have to say to us today?

The author of the book of Chronicles described the fifth century before Jesus (the 400s). The writer interpreted ancient Israel's history very simply in terms of fidelity and infidelity. God repeatedly asked the Hebrews to be faithful to the covenantal promises they had made, and the Hebrews repeatedly broke these promises. So the author interpreted the tragedies of ancient Israel in light of their infidelities. That's why, the author wrote, ancient Babylonia conquered Israel in the sixth century. But eventually God freed the Hebrews from their oppressors through a king of Persia, who let the Hebrews return to their homeland.

The author here described God's care for ancient Israel not only in their triumphs but especially in their tragedies. And the author challenged us to trust in God's care for us in the midst of our own bad luck.

In his letter to the Christian community in Ephesus, Paul described God's graciousness or goodness to us. God through Jesus Christ, crucified and risen, by the power of the Spirit has graced or gifted us with his friendship so we can participate in God's life here and fully in that life beyond this earthly life. Paul here challenged us to remember our ultimate purpose: eternal life with God beyond this earthly life.

In the Gospel according to John, the author described a conversation between Jesus and Nicodemus. The author played on the theme of light and darkness. Nicodemus here recognized Jesus as one who had come from God.

Then Jesus used an image to capture the meaning of his own life. Just as Moses lifted up an image of a snake on a pole so that all who looked on it could be saved, so Jesus had to be lifted up on a cross so all could have eternal life. Jesus is indeed our Savior, our way, our truth, and our light.

During these lenten days, I invite you to reflect on the four recognized Gospels and their faces or portraits of Jesus so you can imitate the virtues Jesus displayed in these Gospels.

Did you ever wonder what Jesus really looked like? You probably heard about the Shroud of Turin. There's a tradition from at least the Middle Ages that says the Shroud has the imprint of the crucified Jesus on the front and back of the cloth. That's one portrait or face of Jesus.

The great painters of our own civilization—Leonardo da Vinci, Raphael, Michelangelo, El Greco, Rembrandt, Rouault, Dali—give us different portraits of Jesus. You may have your own favorite portrait of him.

In describing Jesus, the four Gospel writers faced a unique challenge. How would they portray someone who was completely human and yet completely divine? Should they overemphasize the divine or the human?

Moreover, the Gospel writers wrote to different audiences, so they wrote differently. So do we. For example, a college student might send a text message to his parents and say. "I spent the whole weekend in the library." To his friends he might text, "I had a blast this weekend."

Which Gospel is most authentic? Which best reflects the historical Jesus? They all do.

Let me focus on two Gospels, Mark and Luke, and the virtues Jesus displayed in them.

Mark was the earliest, written circa AD 70, shortly after scores of Christians in Rome perished during the persecution by the emperor Nero. Many Christians were asking, where is God in the midst of our sufferings? And possibly because so many disciples were being martyred, Mark thought he ought to write down who Jesus was, what he did, and what he taught. By the way, tradition has it that Mark was a companion of Peter, a good source of information.

Mark is an action Gospel. The Jesus in Mark seems very approachable, a very human Jesus. We can easily relate to the feelings of Jesus. He was compassionate with the handicapped and tough with hypocrites. He felt misunderstood by the disciples, angry in the temple with the buyers and traders, afraid in the garden of Gethsemane, and abandoned on the cross. Yes, the Jesus in Mark is the Messiah who suffered so we can live forever. What happened to Jesus, Mark says, can happen to us too. To be a disciple, for Mark, may mean enduring sufferings, making sacrifices, and giving generously to other people—for example, our families, friends, colleagues, and yes, even strangers.

Luke gave us still another portrait of Jesus. Luke wasn't an eyewitness. He was a Greek convert who wrote to Gentile Christians much like himself. He gave women a prominent role in his Gospel. Salvation is for everyone, Jews as well as Gentiles. He also emphasized the Spirit.

Luke saw Jesus as a friend and advocate of the poor, the handicapped; he was incredibly compassionate toward the so-called social outcasts. The Jesus in Luke was also forgiving. Remember the parable of the prodigal son. Even on the cross Jesus prayed, "Father, forgive them."

Yes, Jesus in Luke is always forgiving and compassionate. To be a disciple for Luke is to be a healer, a reconciler, a peacemaker; someone who tries to break down the barriers that divide people. Above all, to be a disciple for Luke is not only to be a hearer of God's word but also like Mary, the disciple par excellence, to be a doer of God's word.

Can we have different portraits or faces of Jesus to inspire us in our lives of discipleship with Jesus? Different ways in which to follow

Jesus—self-sacrifice or generosity in Mark; forgiveness, healing, and peacemaking in Luke? Yes, of course. Jesus, the God-man, is more than any one person can adequately describe in human language.

And so the question we might ask this lenten season is, how can I better reflect in my behavior and attitudes the attributes or virtues of Jesus highlighted in the Gospels of Mark and Luke? And so I invite you to meditate on the Gospels this lenten season, for they give us portraits of Jesus that underscore the virtues Jesus displayed, virtues worthy of imitation in the pursuit of our lives of discipleship with Jesus.

Fifth Sunday in Lent

I'm considering carefully the length of my homily in light of a youngster's book report. It consisted of three sentences: "Socrates was a philosopher. He talked a lot. They killed him."

How many are enjoying March basketball madness? We all like winners. You may have heard about the army general who went to a luncheon and ordered a broiled lobster. When the lobster was brought out, it was minus a claw, so he summoned the waiter.

The waiter said, "General, let me explain. All our lobsters are kept in a holding tank. While they're in the tank, they often fight and sometimes lose a claw."

And the general shouted back, "Then for God's sake, bring me a winner." Yes, I guess we all like winners.

This fifth Sunday in the lenten season, the word of God takes us back in our imaginations to the sixth century before Jesus (the 500s) and to a man by the name of Jeremiah, known to many as Mr. Doom and Gloom.

But, in fact, Jeremiah was an optimist. The sixth century was a catastrophe for the Hebrews. Babylonia conquered Israel, murdered the king, devastated the city of Jerusalem, tore down the temple, and deported many Hebrews to Babylonia. In the midst of this catastrophe, Jeremiah dreamed about a new covenant with God, a new friendship with God summed up in that simple-yet-profound phrase "You are my people and I am your God."

This covenant would be written in their hearts. The covenant promises would be kept. Jeremiah challenged us to be faithful to our baptismal promises, to ask at the start of every day for the grace to live as sons and daughters of God, disciples of Jesus. The author of the letter to the Hebrews spoke about the saving work of Jesus Christ.

Jesus is completely human and completely divine—that is the mystery of the incarnation. And this Jesus, through his dying and rising, has rescued us from death, from nothingness, and has opened up to us new possibilities of life beyond this earthly life through eternal life. And Jesus, already transfigured into a new heavenly reality, anticipates our own new heavenly reality. This Word challenges us to remember our ultimate purpose: salvation or eternal life with God and our fellow human beings.

In the Gospel according to John, Jesus was in Jerusalem for the Jewish Passover meal, which celebrates the exodus, the rescue or deliverance, of the Hebrews from their oppressors in Ancient Egypt. Here in Jerusalem Gentiles, non-Jews, are seeking Jesus out. They want to see him. And to see Jesus, for the author, is to believe in him. Yes, the hour has come. Only by the dying of Jesus will we come to life. That is the point of the parable about the grain of wheat.

Only if Jesus is lifted up on a cross, lifted up from the grave and up to his Father, will he draw all men and women to himself into a new heavenly reality. And just as religious Jews will celebrate the passage of their forebears from oppression to freedom, so too do we celebrate Jesus's passage or Passover from death to life at the Easter vigil: a passage that liberates us from death and nothingness, and gifts us with God's life.

Yes, Jesus is indeed our Savior. He is indeed our salvation. But what does salvation mean?

We live in a culture that advertises countless phony forms of salvation. We see ads for everything from expensive cosmetic surgeries to the latest drugs. Yes, we are told these will save us—from old age, anxiety, obesity, pain or illness, or whatever ... We will look and feel better only if we do this or take that.

And then there are bumper stickers that say, "Jesus saves." But again, from what? In the Gospels, Jesus "saves" when he heals, forgives, rescues, and satisfies our spiritual hunger.

For Saint Paul, salvation meant we possess within ourselves, by virtue of the waters of baptism, God's grace, the gift of God's triune life. Paul used several words to describe salvation: *liberation, justification,* or *a right relationship with God.* That was salvation for Paul: the gift of God's triune life within us, God's grace.

Salvation is really a lifelong process, not a quick fix that happens in an instant like some fundamentalist preachers may say. We continually have to struggle against the darkness within us.

The word *salvation* tries to answer a fundamental question: what is the ultimate purpose of my life? Whether we are powerful or powerless, rich or poor, brilliant or dull, American or Asian, the purpose of life is to be in a relationship with God. That's why we are here: to be in a relationship and friendship with God forever.

The Catholic answer to the question "Why are we here?" acknowledges the brevity and fragility of human life. It also acknowledges our freedom to choose good over evil, right over wrong, the true over the false. And vice versa, unfortunately. Hence all of us are responsible, accountable for the way in which we choose to live.

Tragically, some people, in fact, do choose evil. And why? Because there's something not quite right with this planet of ours. Some governments continue to deny people their basic human rights. People are doing violence to one another in countries around the world. The Catholic tradition calls this "original sin": the tendency or pull within us to sometimes choose wrong over right; this is a lack of a genuine relationship with God. Human beings cry out for healing, redemption, and salvation.

But who can heal us? Who can save us? Some, of course, have sought human solutions to this human problem. They have looked for answers in the world of things, in other persons, and in the great twentieth-century "isms" of one kind or another.

The Catholic tradition looks beyond the world of things to a power beyond us, a God who isn't indifferent to our brokenness, our alienation. For our God is an all-good God.

This God became flesh in Jesus of Nazareth and is alive by the power of the Spirit and is in our midst today—alive within us by virtue of the waters of baptism; alive in our midst in the scriptures and in the signs of bread and wine on this altar. Yes, we possess within our fragile selves

God's triune life, God's grace. We are in a relationship with God. But we must continue to struggle against the forces within us that try to fracture that relationship and derail us on our journey toward God.

Salvation ultimately means God's triune life within us forever. And I pray that, as we hear the words of the author of Jeremiah, Hebrews, and John today, we will reenergize ourselves to seek God first in our everyday lives, that we will recharge and reenergize ourselves.

And how do we do this? By renewing our baptismal promises continually, especially at Easter; by changing our hearts; and by turning away every day from a self-centered life to a God-centered, other-centered one.

Palm Sunday

Our Christian community on Ash Wednesday invited us to treat ourselves to those age-old exercises of prayer, fasting (or doing without so that others can have), and almsgiving (or sharing our time, talents, and treasures with others) so we can deepen our relationship with God and our fellow human beings.

I hope your exercises during the lenten season have been invigorating. Today we begin Holy Week, the chief week of the liturgical year. We focus in particular on the paschal mystery (the dying and rising of Jesus Christ) or the journey of Jesus from this earthly life through the mystery of death into a transformative heavenly life.

Now the word *paschal* refers to the Hebrew Passover or the passing of the angel of death over the homes of the Hebrews in Ancient Egypt (a passing over that spared their firstborn child from death). In a larger sense, the Passover refers to the exodus or liberation of the Hebrews from their oppressors; and every year the Jewish community re-experiences this exodus or liberation in the so-called seder service, which they celebrate at sunset.

This Palm Sunday we reflect on a paradox of triumph and tragedy: the triumphal entry of Jesus into Jerusalem on the one hand and the Gospel proclamation of the passion and death of Jesus on the other. And even in the tragedy of Good Friday, there is the triumph of Easter: Jesus crucified, risen, and in our midst.

The word of God from Isaiah is a poem about a servant who suffers for us (the early Christian community saw Jesus in this servant). Paul's letter to the Christian community at Philippi quotes an early Christian hymn about God who became one of us. And the Gospel according to Mark proclaims the passion and death of Jesus.

Next Thursday, Friday, and Saturday are known as the triduum (from a Latin word that means "a period of three days"). On Thursday we will commemorate the Lord's Supper. There is the washing of feet (a symbol of service) and then the eating of a meal—a sacrificial meal—in which Jesus gives himself to us in the signs of bread and wine (a symbol of our oneness not only with God but also with our fellow human beings). On Good Friday we meditate on the passion and death of Jesus, including the garden of Gethsemane, the trial, the crucifixion, the burial, the veneration of the cross, and then a simple Communion service.

And at the Easter vigil we will reflect on the passage of Jesus from this earthly life through death into a transformative heavenly life; the resurrection of Jesus is a pledge of our own liberation from death or nothingness into eternal life. The vigil includes fire (a symbol of Jesus as the Light who illuminates the darkness around us), the proclamation of the story of our salvation in the scriptures, the renewal of our baptismal promises, and the Eucharist. Easter proclaims that Jesus is risen and alive among us, especially alive in the sacramental life of our Catholic community. This is indeed the chief week of the Catholic liturgical year, and I urge all of you to participate in these services as much as you can.

Let me conclude with a story about a German ship, the *Deutschland*, which ran aground on a shoal four miles off the coast of England in 1875. Unlike the *Titanic*, the *Deutschland* had enough lifeboats and life preservers for everyone. But they did the passengers no good. The fierce gale winds swamped the boats, and the passengers were told to go to the deck. Although the passengers could see the lights of the English shore, no one there saw the ship's distress signals.

Among the 157 passengers who perished were five Franciscan nuns traveling to Missouri for a new teaching ministry. They were immortalized in a poem, to which I will allude in a moment. These five nuns, fleeing Otto von Bismarck's anti-Catholic legislation in 1873, stayed below deck because there wasn't enough room for them on the deck. The poem reads,

"As the water rose around them,
they clasped hands and were heard saying,
'O Christ, O Christ, come quickly!'"

The newspaper accounts of this tragedy profoundly moved the English Jesuit poet Gerard Manley Hopkins, who wrote a poem about it, "The Wreck of the Deutschland." He dedicated the poem to these five Franciscan nuns. He saw in their deaths a parallel to the sufferings of Jesus for the sake of the many. Hopkins concluded the poem with this line referring to Christ: "Let him easter in us, be a dayspring to the dimness of us."

As used in this poem, the word *easter* is a nautical term that means steering a craft toward the east into the light. And that Light is Jesus Christ. Yes, "let [Christ] easter in us" so we may reflect his life by practicing virtue—for example, through compassion, peacemaking, justice, truth, and forgiveness. "Let [Christ] easter in us" that he may empower us to be healers, teachers, and foot washers like him. "Let [Christ] easter in us" so that he may give us courage to bear our crosses as he bore his cross for us. "Let him easter in us" so that, at the end of our earthly voyage, Christ may carry us away within himself forever.

Yes, throughout these forty days of Lent, we have been trying to steer our lives toward the light of Jesus Christ and to shake off the darkness around us and the burdens of our daily lives. And I pray that this Holy Week will inspire us to seek ever more enthusiastically the God who became flesh in Jesus of Nazareth, who by his death and resurrection opened up to all humankind a transformative eternal life beyond this earthly life. And then in the moment of our own dying, we, like those five Franciscan nuns in the poem, will be able to pray, "O Christ, O Christ, come quickly so that you can 'easter' or live in us as our light forever."

Easter

Happy Easter! *Felices Pascuas! Joyeuses Paques! Buona Pasqua!*
The word *Easter* comes from Eastre, the name of a Saxon goddess
of the dawn or spring. And Easter symbolizes life. Jesus is alive! Proclaim
it in your home languages!

Easter brings back childhood memories. We used to dye or color eggs
with designs. The egg symbolizes hope and life. And just as the small

chick at birth breaks out from its narrow world in the shell into a much bigger world, so too we believe that in the mystery of our own dying, we will break out of our own earthly "skin," so to speak, into a newly transfigured heavenly life.

These memories of childhood remind me of David Heller's paperback *Dear God: Children's Letters to God.* For example,

> Dear God, Thank you for my parents, my sister Anita, and for my grandma and grandpa. I forgive you for my brother Phil. I guess you didn't finish working on him.

Or,

> Dear God, My dad thinks he is you. Please straighten him out.

Youngsters can be so funny.

I heard about some youngsters who were lined up in the school cafeteria. At the beginning of the line, there was a large pile of apples with a note stating, "Take only ONE. God is watching." And at the other end of the line, there was a large pile of chocolate chip cookies. And a youngster wrote a note. "Take all you want. God is watching the apples." So much for youngsters.

In the word of God today, Peter proclaimed the kerygma, the proclamation of the good news. He spoke about all God has done for us through Jesus of Nazareth. John baptized Jesus in the Jordan River; he was anointed with the Spirit and went about the countryside of Judea and Galilee, working signs and wonders, proclaiming that the kingdom of God was breaking into our midst. Eventually Jesus was crucified but then lifted up out of the tomb and lifted up to his heavenly Father so he could draw us to himself in a new, transfigured heavenly life.

Yes, Jesus is alive, and because he lives, we also live. He is indeed, Peter shouted, a God of mercy and forgiveness. And that's why Pope Francis emphasizes so often that the church is a field hospital, here to heal wounds.

In his letter to the Christian community in Colossae, Turkey, Paul challenged us to seek God in our everyday lives so we might appear with him in glory at the End Times. And in the Gospel according to John, we hear the story of the resurrection of Jesus. Mary Magdalene went to the tomb only to find it empty; she was frightened and summoned Peter and John, who went in while she stayed outside. Yes, the disciples discovered that Jesus wasn't among the dead. He is risen; he is alive. He passed from this earthly life through the mystery of death into a new, transfigured heavenly reality. And this future is ours as well.

Some of you may know I went to college in Washington, DC. Every now and then I went back to Washington, and when I had time, I made my way to the Vietnam Memorial, a simple yet immensely moving tribute.

The two arms of the long, V-shaped polished black granite wall point toward the Washington Monument on one side and the Lincoln Memorial on the other. And on the wall are inscribed more than fifty-eight thousand names of men and women killed or still missing from the Vietnam War. Sometimes I found and read a letter at the foot of that wall that a son or daughter had written home. And I often thought, *How many hopes lie buried here for that family?* The soldiers were full of life, with so many dreams. And suddenly they were dead.

And then I thought about Easter. The disciples of Jesus, huddled in the upper room in Jerusalem, could have said the same thing: about how many hopes lay buried here. The disciples who met Jesus on the road to Emmaus said practically the same thing. And yet some forty hours after those hopes were buried, the risen Christ appeared to the disciples: to Mary Magdalene, the disciples in the upper room, and the disciples on the road to Emmaus.

Jesus wasn't simply a spirit or ghost; nor was he simply resuscitated. Otherwise they would have recognized him immediately; he couldn't have disappeared so easily from the upper room. Yes, it was a bodily resurrection; the earthly and crucified Jesus was the same person as the resurrected Jesus. The earthly body of Jesus was transfigured or transformed into a new reality. Jesus said to the disciples, "I live and you will live." (John 14:19) But how is that?

No sooner are we born in the flesh than we are reborn in the spirit. Water is poured on us in the rite of baptism, and in these waters the

Spirit of God is poured out on us, and a new life is ours: the life of the triune God. What a tremendous reality this is. The God of this universe lives within us by virtue of baptism. We carry within us the very spark of the divine. And as we grow into adolescence, the bishop anoints our foreheads with oil in the sign of the cross, and in that gesture God empowers us to live out the demands of discipleship.

At Eucharist, where Jesus sacramentally presences himself to us in the signs of bread and wine, and mystically reenacts his redemptive, salvific activity and becomes one with us ever so briefly in communion, the living Christ feeds us with his life so we can continue our journey. And if we should ever lose this, the living Christ is ready to restore it in the rite of penance, where we celebrate God's mercy. Yes, through the sacraments, privileged encounters with God, we experience the living Christ. In the exchange of wedding promises strengthening that love between husband and wife, Christ is a partner. In the anointing of the sick, Christ makes our passage easier. All the sacraments are indeed concrete, visible signs of God's care for us.

Life with God in a new, transformative, heavenly reality—that is the ultimate purpose. Someday this earthly body of ours, like that of Jesus, will be transformed. At every Funeral Mass we hear, "For those who believe, life is not taken away; life is merely changed." That is the Easter message. That is the song of Easter. Praise the Lord!

Our Easter faith proclaims loudly and clearly that the eternal life Jesus won for us through his death and resurrection, that divine life bestowed on us in baptism and nourished in the sacramental life of the community, won't disappear in the mystery of death. No, the risen Christ promises us that we will make an evolutionary leap into a new reality.

And so let every morning, like that first Easter morning, be a morning to start over, to begin again. Perhaps the night before, we carried the burdens of the day just completed: things left undone, bad things said, good things left unsaid. But whatever was yesterday is done.

Ours is a morning faith: starting over, beginning again. Who among us is content with who we are? Who among us doesn't know a heart to heal, a relationship to mend, or a lost soul to find? Easter proclaims it's a new day, a new season, a new life.

Second Sunday of Easter

I just heard about a husband and wife who traveled to Israel for their fiftieth wedding anniversary. Unfortunately, in Jerusalem the wife suddenly died. The funeral director told her husband, Moses, that he could bury Miriam in Israel for $100, but in the United States, it would cost $10,000 (flying the body home and so forth).

Moses had had a turbulent and stormy marriage with Miriam.

He considered for a moment and decided to bury her in the United States. The funeral director, perplexed, asked why. Moses said, "I heard that someone died here almost two thousand years ago, and he rose from the dead. I want to be sure Miriam is buried once and for all, so I'll bury her in the US, even if it costs ten thousand dollars."

How many of you remember the Academy Award–winning film *March of the Penguins?* The film describes a fascinating phenomenon. All summer the emperor penguins in Antarctica feast on fish. Then in the fall, as if on cue, these stately, plump birds leave the ocean and trek seventy miles to their breeding ground. Thousands of penguins, marching single file, waddle to the same icy valley where every one of them was born.

When they arrive, the penguins choose mates. This is no casual commitment. The mother penguin lays a single egg, and the father gathers it into the feathery folds below his large stomach to protect it from the cold and ice. The mother penguins then go to the sea to forage for food. For two months, the fathers stand—with no food or water, in howling gales and temperatures far below zero, and in darkness—each protecting an egg.

To keep warm, the thousands of birds huddle together, taking turns moving from the outer edges to the center of the flock. And then in the spring, the eggs that have survived the winter hatch. Father and chick then await the return of the mother. How do these thousands of penguins, who apparently look exactly alike, reunite with their mates and chicks (chicks the mothers have never seen)? Each penguin family has developed its own unique vocal signature. They are reunited by listening for their family amid a crowd of penguin cries, whistles, and pipes.

As you watch *March of the Penguins*, you may feel a certain kinship with these birds, who endure all kinds of physical hardships for the sake of their families. Their so-called family commitment to one another reflects a parent's love for his or her children and a desire to love unconditionally, regardless of the cost, and to love even when it may not be acknowledged and appreciated.

Now what does *March of the Penguins* have to do with the word of God just proclaimed? The book of the Acts of the Apostles carries us back in our imaginations to the beginnings of Christianity, to a faith community that shared what they had with one another. They were a family who looked out for one another and cared deeply about one another.

The letter of John emphasizes what unites us as a spiritual family: our faith in Jesus Christ, our spiritual birth in the waters of baptism, our sharing sacramentally in the body and blood of Jesus Christ, and our fidelity to a particular ethical way of life. As Mother Teresa said simply but profoundly, "God does not ask us to be successful, but to be faithful: to our relationships, and to our responsibilities."

In the Gospel according to John, we find a postresurrection appearance of Jesus to the disciples. We have no idea what the risen body of Jesus looked like—a body that could pass through the barred doors of an upper room just as he penetrated the sealed rock door of his tomb. And in this passage the risen Jesus bestowed on the disciples, through the power and energy of the Spirit, the gifts of wisdom, love, courage, peace, and forgiveness.

The skeptical Thomas wasn't there that day. Lo and behold, a week later Jesus appeared again. And then Thomas made his declaration with the eyes of faith: "My Lord and My God."

Thomas's declaration of faith should be ours. Yes, we with the eyes of faith see in Jesus our Lord and our God who unites us as a spiritual family. Let's reflect on family life, a happy family.

1. Happy families have a good, solid sense of togetherness. They feel a closeness with one another; they care about one another. They keep in touch, even if it's by e-mail, text messaging, or telephone. They're hospitable and concerned about elderly relatives. They remember birthdays and anniversaries, and celebrate them. They participate in special family events: graduations, baptisms, confirmations, marriages, and so forth. They take responsibility for family chores. They spend time together; they set times to eat meals together. They share the good news as well as the bad. They keep their word and thereby build up trust.

2. Happy families don't let outside activities control them; they control activities. As someone put it, "How can we enjoy one another if we never see one another?"

3. Parents have to let each child become the person God created him or her to be. Yes, they need guidance, but we shouldn't force them to live out our dreams. The purpose of family is to nurture children in a secure and loving environment until they become mature enough to venture out on their own and become responsible persons.

4. In all our relationships, avoid negative, judgmental words; always distinguish the behavior we find objectionable from judgments about the person. For example, someone is late. A negative judgment would be "You never think about anyone but yourself." The actual behavior is "You're late; maybe there was a car accident. Address the behavior and avoid blurting out negative judgments that subtly undermine a relationship. All relationships call for nurturing if they are to grow.

Marian Wright Edelman, a children's advocate and author, wrote this examination of conscience for us:

> If we're not supporting a child we brought into the world as a father or as a mother with attention, time, love discipline, money and the teaching of virtues; If we spend more time worrying about our children's clothes than about their character; If we think it's someone else's responsibility to teach our children virtues, respect, good manners, and work and health habits; If we believe the Sermon on the Mount and the Ten Commandments pertain only to Sunday but not to our Monday through Saturday home, professional, and political life; And if we think being American is about how much we can get rather than how much we can give and if we think that things and not character make the person; Then we are a part of the problem rather than the solution.

As we reflect on the theme of family in scripture, let us think of ways to draw our family closer: nurture togetherness, manage our schedules, let children become the persons God created them to be, and address behavior rather than make negative judgments about people. And if we try to do these things, then we'll discover an even happier family life.

Surely we can care for our loved ones just as much as the penguins care for theirs.

Third Sunday of Easter

The baseball season is in full swing, and here's a question for you. Do we have any Tampa Bay Rays fans? You may know about the intense rivalry between Yankees and Red Sox fans, and I read a story that highlights that rivalry.

Two youngsters were playing baseball in Central Park in Manhattan when a rabid dog attacked the smaller of the two. Thinking quickly, the other youngster grabbed some rope, lassoed the dog, and tied it to a tree until help arrived.

A *New York Post* reporter saw the incident and ran over to interview the young hero. The reporter began to write, "Young Yankees Fan Saves Friend from Vicious Dog."

"But I'm not a Yankees fan," the youngster pointed out.

So the reporter said, "Mets Fan Rescues Friend from Rabid Dog."

"But, sir, I really don't like the Mets either," the youngster said.

And so the reporter said, "I figured everyone in NYC was either a Yankees or a Mets fan. So what team do you root for?"

"The Red Sox," the youngster answered.

The reporter began a new page in his notebook with the following lead: "Ruthless Child Almost Chokes Beloved Family Pet to Death."

I guess the moral of the story is that we shouldn't mess with *New York Post* reporters about the Yankees or Mets. They take their baseball seriously.

I begin with a story about someone who stood up for what he believed was right. Some of you in the medical profession may have heard of Dr. Ignaz

Semmelweis. He's responsible for one of the most important procedures in health care, and the discovery cost him a great medical career.

Dr. Semmelweis was an obstetrician in nineteenth-century Vienna, Austria. He found that one mother in ten died from infection while in the hospital. As he observed procedures, he began to suspect that the doctors were causing infections. He suggested that they wash their hands with antiseptic before they touched the mothers.

The doctors were outraged. How dare this young "doctor nobody" tell experienced physicians what to do? But Semmelweis insisted. And when the doctors started washing their hands with antiseptic, the deaths stopped. This simple step, now standard procedure, saved lives. Yet instead of being saluted, Semmelweis was forced out of the hospital and out of Austria.

The point of this story is simple enough: faith demands courage; standing up for something you believe is right, true, and good can be risky. As Dr. Semmelweis unfortunately discovered, standing up for what was right created conflict, though it saved lives.

Peter and the other disciples found out that standing up for their beliefs was risky. In fact, it eventually cost them their lives. And every one of us as a disciple of Jesus is called to stand up for what is right, true, and good, for we believe that love rather than hate, right rather than wrong, truth rather than falsehood, and forgiveness rather than vengeance are virtues worth standing up for.

The word of God, just proclaimed, highlights how God gifted Peter with faith and courage so he could proclaim the good news, the kerygma, that the God of Abraham, Isaac, and Jacob raised Jesus up from death. This Jesus is indeed the holy and righteous One, the author of life, and the long-awaited Messiah of the Jews.

Then Peter concluded, "Repent." Refocus your lives upon God, seek forgiveness and mercy, and ask for God's grace so that God's light within you can shine through your daily activities.

The letter of John proclaims that we have a Father in heaven; hence we are sons and daughters of God, heirs to the kingdom of God. And Jesus Christ is our advocate and mediator, the One through whom God gifts us with his eternal life. But to participate in God's life, we must be not only hearers but also doers of God's word.

And in the Gospel according to Luke, two disciples told the other disciples about their extraordinary experience. During the breaking of the bread at Emmaus, they recognized with their eyes of faith the new, transformed reality of Jesus Christ. And as they recounted this experience, Jesus suddenly appeared in their midst, showed them the marks on his hands and feet, and ate with them. Yes, God transformed the earthly Jesus into a new, indescribable, transcendent reality; and so, too, God will transform us into a new, transcendent reality in the mystery of our own death. And then the disciples proclaimed the good news with faith and courage that Jesus Christ is alive, and because he lives, you and I live.

To be a disciple of Jesus is to be fundamentally a man or woman of faith, someone who trusts completely in an all-good God in our earthly journey to our heavenly home, someone who tries to do what God wants us to do, even though we can't always seem to figure out what precisely that is. But the gift of faith has to be nurtured continually. Let me highlight four simple practices or disciplines whereby we can nurture our faith. Some call these "the four S's."

1. Slow down. It's so important to take at least fifteen minutes a day to tune into the presence of God as we go about our daily routines. People find all sorts of ways to tune in: a daily walk or run, a stop at a church, a quiet moment in the car. Yes, take time to slow down so you can tune into the presence of God. And on the weekend, gather as often as you can with your faith community to celebrate liturgy or mass.

2. Study wisdom. All of us should be lifelong learners. Study the Bible. There are so many easy-to-use Bible study tools available today. And study the teachings of the church with a resource such as the *Catechism of the Catholic Church*. There are many other resources—for example, catalogs or sites on the web, including such sites as Americancatholic.org.

3. Serve others. The Gospels are filled with examples of Jesus serving others. We too are called to serve in our families,

workplaces, local communities, and beyond. Maybe you've heard the phrase "Think globally, act locally." Engage, for example, in a parish volunteer ministry. Work at a soup kitchen, Catholic charity, St. Vincent de Paul, or Habitat for Humanity. Become an advocate for the poor at the local, state, or national level. And remember: serving begins in your own home.

4. Share your faith with others. A disciple talks about his or her faith. It can be as simple as asking or reflecting with others on the work we do. How can we better reflect in our own workplace values or virtues such as honesty, integrity, responsibility, friendship, courage, perseverance, compassion, loyalty, faith in God, and a respect for colleagues.

The point is this. Our faith is a gift, but like a flower in a garden, it must be fed and cared for. And so remember the four S's: slow down to tune into the presence of God, study the wisdom of the Bible and the church, serve at home and in the community, and share your faith with others. These four simple yet rigorous practices will help us keep the flame of faith alive within us.

Fourth Sunday of Easter

During the presidential campaigns, I happened to see a 1990s best seller titled *The Death of Common Sense* by Philip Howard. The point of this best seller is that too many government regulations have replaced common sense.

The BBC even ran an "obituary" about the death of common sense. Here are a few excerpts: "Common sense will be remembered for cultivating such valuable lessons as: knowing when to come in out of the rain; why the early bird gets the worm; life isn't always fair; maybe it was my fault; and don't spend more than you earn."

The obituary went on to say, "The health of Common Sense began to deteriorate rapidly when well-intentioned but overbearing regulations were set in place. Common Sense finally gave up the will to live after someone failed to realize that a steaming hot cup of coffee was hot. She spilled a little, and was awarded a huge settlement. Not many attended the funeral of Common Sense because so few realized he was gone." The point is that many things are simply a matter of good judgment and common sense. Yes, let's hope our candidates bring common sense back into our political arena.

Now the word of God, just proclaimed, carries us back in our imaginations to the beginnings of Christianity, to the apostles Peter and John. They were both arrested—Peter for doing a good deed—in other words, healing a crippled man in the name of Jesus. I can't help but think of the axiom "No good deed goes unpunished."

In this passage Peter courageously proclaimed that Jesus Christ is the cornerstone or foundation of a new age and that we have access to God's triune life through the death and resurrection of Jesus.

The author of the Acts of the Apostles may have been asking us whether Jesus is indeed the cornerstone or foundation of our own lives—in other words, our way to eternal life, our truth who sets us free from falsehoods, and our Light who illumines our darkness.

The letter of John speaks about our future. God is our Father, and we are God's sons and daughters. Yes, one day we shall see God as he is; yes, we shall be like God. We might ask, "Do we realize that we are sons and daughters of God and, as such, called to do the will of God in our everyday lives?"

In the Gospel according to John, we have the image of Jesus as the Good Shepherd. Now I'm a Brooklyn boy and can't seem to relate easily to shepherds and sheep. In fact, I wouldn't have sheep as pets; I hear they're smelly. Moreover, I don't identify life with sheep and shepherds but with computers, tablets, and smartphones. You and I live in a tech-information age.

But as someone wrote, life is not based only on information about God but also on experiences of God. Jesus's audience could easily relate to shepherds and sheep. There are many images or metaphors about Jesus in John's Gospel: bread, vine, sheep gate, the way, the truth, the life, and shepherd. I doubt anyone here has been a sheepherder. We may have to go out of state to watch sheepherders with dog and horse keeping the sheep together, moving them about for food and water, and protecting them from wolves.

Ancient shepherds had to work even harder: they had no horse, dog, or modern weapon. And the job was dangerous. They had to deal not only with wild animals but also with outlaws and rustlers.

The shepherd's dedication to the sheep inspired the biblical writers to speak about God as a Good Shepherd. Thus the psalmist sang, "The Lord is my shepherd." (Psalms 23:1) Like the good shepherd in ancient Israel, Jesus cared for the weak and helpless, healed the sick, brought back the stray, and sought out the lost sheep. Yes, he did even more: he lay down his life for his sheep. We may be wondering, *Where are the "good shepherds" today? In corporations, politics, churches, sports?*

Yes, the word of God today gives us much to think about. I would like to zero in on the letter of John. The author said God is our Father and that we are sons and daughters of God, and as such, we are called to do the "will of God" in our everyday lives.

But how do we do the "will of God?" Isn't the "will of God" often vague, ambiguous, and unclear? Yes and no.

I believe we do the "will of God" by being faithful in our relationships and responsibilities, and by doing the best we can as we go about our everyday activities. Think about it. If you're a parent working to pay the bills but making time to be with your children when they need you, you're doing the will of God. If you're overwhelmed by the care of a dying spouse, a sick child, or an elderly parent but try your best to make a loving home for him or her, blessed are you. You're doing the will of God.

If you happily give your time to work at a soup kitchen, shop for a neighbor who's housebound, help a youngster with a classroom assignment, blessed are you. If you befriend the unpopular, the perpetually lost, blessed are you. If you refuse to take shortcuts when it comes to doing what is right, if you refuse to compromise your integrity and ethics, and refuse to take refuge in the rationalization that "Everybody does it," blessed are you. You're doing the will of God.

If you try to understand things from the perspective of the other person and manage to find a way to make things work for the good; if you're feeling discouraged and frustrated because you are worrying, waiting, bending over backward, paying the price for loving the unlovable, and forgiving the undeserving, blessed are you.

If you struggle to discover what God asks of you in all things, if you try to seek God's presence in every facet of your life and every decision you make, if your constant prayer isn't "Give me" but "Help me," blessed are you. You're doing the will of God.

If you readily spend time listening and consoling others who look to you for support, for guidance, for compassion; if you manage to heal wounds and build bridges; if others see in you goodness, graciousness, joy, and serenity; if you can see the good in everyone and seek the good for everyone, blessed are you.

If you are rejected or demeaned because of your background, if your faith puts you at odds with some people, and if you refuse to compromise basic principles to simply "get along," blessed are you. You're doing the will of God. And in the end, heaven will be yours.

My friends, the word of God invites us to think about many things: Jesus Christ as the cornerstone or center of our lives in the book of Acts; our purpose in life, which is seeing God face-to-face in the letter of John; and Jesus as our Good Shepherd in the Gospels.

Jesus calls us to eternal life and asks us to seek the will of God in our daily lives. May God grace us to do so. And then we will indeed see God face-to-face.

Fifth Sunday of Easter

I read the story about a few people who want to take God out of the Pledge of Allegiance.

The story says, "With earthquakes in Nepal, tornados in Texas, volcanic eruptions in Chile, wars in the Middle East, droughts in California, boats with migrants capsizing in the Mediterranean and the threat of terrorist attacks everywhere, does anyone think this is a good time to take God out of the Pledge of Allegiance?"

I don't think so. What do you think?

The word of God in the book of the Acts of the Apostles describes how Paul, once a fierce persecutor, was introduced to the Christian community in Jerusalem. Paul was a devout Jew, a rabbi who suddenly on the road to Damascus in Syria had a visionary experience of the living Christ. That experience turned Paul's life upside down. He went from fierce persecutor to great evangelizer of Christianity. And thereafter, his one passion in life was to proclaim everywhere he went the good news or gospel: Jesus is alive! And because he lives, we live—in God's triune life. Paul traveled by land and sea, overcame the obstacles he met in the cities of the eastern Mediterranean, was jailed for creating controversies, founded churches in Turkey and Greece, wrote letters to these communities, and eventually was martyred in Rome.

The vision that fired Paul up was this: Paul wrote to the Christian community at Ephesus that God gave him the "amazing grace" to see God's plan for all humankind. And at the center of God's plan for us is

Jesus Christ, the eternal Word who became flesh in Jesus, the mystery of the incarnation.

For Paul, Jesus was the image of the invisible God, and in him all things hold together.

Paul's writings remind me of the fire-and-brimstone preacher who described how he prepares his sermons: "First I read myself full, I think myself clear, I pray myself hot, and I let myself go."

Paul could have written the prayer of the nineteenth-century British theologian Blessed John Henry Newman:

> God has committed some work to me which He has not committed to another. I have my mission. I shall do good, I shall do His work... Therefore I will trust God. If I am in sickness, my sickness may serve Him; in perplexity, my perplexity may serve Him; in sorrow, my sorrow may serve Him. God may prolong my life, He may shorten it; He knows what He is about. He may take away my friends, He may throw me among strangers, He may make me feel desolate, make my spirits sink, hide the future from me—still God knows what He is about.

That prayer of Blessed John Newman should be ours as well, because God has created us to do him some definite service.

The author of the letter of John goes to the heart of the matter. The truth is found in Jesus, the Son of God; and to believe in Jesus is to love our fellow human beings. We love God to the extent we love and care for one another.

And in the Gospel according to John, the author described, in the metaphor of a vine and branches, the relationship of Jesus to you and me and all Christians. Just as branches can't bear fruit unless they are connected to the vine, so we, too, cannot do good works unless we are connected to the living Christ.

Yes, living Christ is the vine, the lifeline to the branches, the global Catholic community today, yesterday, and tomorrow. This is a community that will push forward until Jesus Christ comes in glory at the End Times. I like three things in particular about the 1.2 billion in the global Catholic community.

First, we remember and celebrate the awesome presence of the living Christ in our midst—Jesus Christ is our way into eternal life, our truth who sets us free from falsehoods, and our Light who scatters our darkness. We retell the stories of Jesus; we celebrate his gestures in the waters of the Jordan, in the upper room of Jerusalem, and at healings in Galilee and Judea. We recognize the presence of God all around us: in an awesome sunrise or sunset; in picturesque landscapes or waterscapes; in courageous people; and in sacramental signs like water, bread, wine, and oil, where we encounter the living Christ. Jesus said, "where two or three are gathered together in my name, there am I in the midst of them." (Matthew 18:20) By the power of the Spirit. That Spirit of fire and wind and energy and power who transformed the disciples from cowards, hiding behind closed doors in Jerusalem, into heroes proclaiming fearlessly on the rooftops that Jesus was alive—that same Spirit lives within this community, within you and me, and can fire us up to do wonders for God if we will only let that Spirit fire us up. That's the first thing I like about belonging to this global Catholic community: we remember and celebrate the awesome presence of the living Christ in our midst.

The second thing I like about belonging to this community is that we are a family. Oh yes, we argue about this or that, but don't all families do that? But in the final analysis, we are a global family that stretches back to early Christianity; and this family will continue into this millennium and perhaps many more millennia until Jesus Christ triumphantly returns in his second coming to transform this universe into a kingdom of peace, justice, and truth.

This family lives under a huge tent, and everyone can fit under it. And yes, some are good, and others are dysfunctional. Yet we have to strive to do what is right, true, and good despite falls or lapses here and there. We need to continually forgive ourselves and one another, let go of those burdens of guilt for behaviors done or not done to others, let go of those feelings of resentment and bitterness for wrongs done to us, and get our lives back on track. Every day should be a fresh start.

And the final thing I like about belonging to the Catholic family is that we do take a stand on peace and justice. I think of the statements of John Paul II, Benedict XVI, and Pope Francis. I think of homeless shelters, hospices, soup kitchens, shelters for battered women, AIDS treatment centers, literacy programs, day care centers, hospitals, and schools all over the world that our Catholic community sponsors.

I also think of international agencies, such as Catholic Relief Services, Caritas International, and the Catholic Agency for Overseas Development, to name but a few, that do so much good for others.

My friends, the image or metaphor of the vine and branches—God in us and we in God— ought to inspire us to always remember that we shall pass through this world but once. Any good therefore we can do or any kindness we can show to any human being, let us do it now. Let us not defer or neglect it, for we shall not pass this way again. And then we truly will live the metaphor of the vine and be branches, branches that bear much fruit.

Sixth Sunday of Easter

Y ou may have heard the story about three professionals (a doctor, teacher, and CEO of an HMO) who died suddenly and appeared at the "heavenly gates."

Saint Peter asked each, "Tell me, what have you done to merit heaven?"

The medical doctor said he worked for "doctors without borders" in underserved countries and performed thousands of surgeries on children. Saint Peter immediately ushered him into heaven. The teacher declared that she'd taught at-risk children in an inner city school for twenty-five years and helped them realize their potential. Saint Peter said, "Well done, welcome into heaven."

The HMO CEO said he'd saved thousands of lives through health insurance. Saint Peter replied, "Welcome to heaven, but you can only stay three days."

Talk about karma.

Today we celebrate Mother's Day, and I invite all mothers to stand for our applause.

The words *mother* and *mom* evoke all kinds of images—for example, homemaker, teacher, nurse, secretary, and chauffeur. Whatever the job, a mother shows her children how to live.

And what is the most important thing a mother can give her children? Unconditional love. Our mothers love us, care for us, coach and mentor us, teach us, are patient with us, and are always ready to listen to us. There is one thing we never will be able to fully "measure," and that is the unconditional love of our mothers. Yes, mothers are truly marvelous, great teachers.

Here are a few things my mother taught me:

Mom taught me to appreciate a job well done. For example, she would say, "If you're going to kill each other, do it outside; I just finished cleaning!"

Mom taught logic. How many have heard their mom say, "Because I said so, that's why!"

And finally Mom taught about envy. She would say, "There are millions of less fortunate kids who don't have the wonderful parents you do!"

Do some of these "lessons" sound familiar to you? Thank you, mothers, for all you do for us.

Mother's Day and Father's Day make me think about all the things parents do for their children. It is indeed "holy work."

What's holy work? I'll tell you. It's looking after the house; getting children to and from school, doctor's appointments, rehearsals, and practices; paying the bills; and balancing the checkbook. These are hardly inspiring, exhilarating experiences. But they are holy acts.

The details—feeding, clothing, cleaning, teaching, driving, coaching, and mentoring—take on a spiritual dimension when they are seen as the mission of helping a child transform into a man or woman of moral character.

For parents, the spiritual isn't ethereal or remote; the holy isn't abstract and confined to words and images. The spiritual is painfully real; the holy is directly connected to the most ordinary and mundane of human activities. It is doing the ordinary extraordinarily well. The spiritual transcends the present to envision the future, and what contributes more to the future than raising a child into a man or woman of moral character? Parenting is indeed a holy vocation.

Now the word of God, just proclaimed, takes us to Peter in the house of Cornelius, a Gentile and, even worse, a Roman centurion. The Romans occupied Jewish lands, and periodically Jews would rebel against the Romans only to be brutally crushed.

And as Peter was proclaiming God's "amazing grace" or salvation or eternal life, the Spirit of God descended on all in the household—Gentiles as well as Jews—and they were baptized into the Christian family.

The word of God reminds us that the Spirit works sometimes in people and places where we least expect to find the Spirit. And so we should always be receptive to God's presence, especially in unlikely people and places, even in our sometimes humdrum homes and daily life.

The authors of the letter of John as well as the Gospel challenge us to love one another as God loves us—unconditionally. Yes, we love God to the extent that we care for one another. Yes, Jesus gave his life for us so we can have God's triune life. Jesus chooses us as friends. And he invites us to nurture that friendship, especially through prayer. The theme of love is an invitation to reflect on our own family life.

Let me first share a true story that is related. Almost a century and a half ago, when diamonds were discovered in Africa, diamond fever quickly spread. Some people struck it rich. But for others, the search became long, arduous, and disappointing. One man sold his farm and wandered throughout the African continent, searching week after week but never finding diamonds.

Meanwhile, back on the land the man had sold, the farmer who had bought the land found a strange-looking stone in a creek on the property. He placed the stone on his fireplace mantle.

One day a visitor noticed it. He grasped the stone quickly and shouted excitedly, "Do you know this is a diamond? It's one of the largest I've ever seen."

They discovered that the entire farm was covered with magnificent diamonds. The point of the story is this: Some people never take the time to notice what they have in their own backyard. Some people never take the time to notice the gems in their own families.

So stop and smell the roses. Look at your family. Yes, right now, look at God's love for your family. See the gem you have in your spouse, your sons or daughters, your parents or grandparents. Any gem, of course, may need some polishing to reveal all the beautiful facets. But they're there.

Erma Bombeck captured the funny in family life in the book *If Life is a Bowl of Cherries, What Am I Doing in the Pits?* The book is about tough love. She wrote that someday, when her children were old enough to understand the logic that motivates a parent, she'd tell them, "I loved you enough to bug you about where you were going, with whom, and what time you would get home. I loved you enough to push you off my lap, let go of your hand ... so you had to stand. And I loved you enough to accept you for what you are, not what I wanted you to be."

Every good parent—every good person—knows that real love is unconditional. Yes, unconditional love, forgiveness, and acceptance. Unconditional love always seeks what is best for someone, even if that someone doesn't think so at that moment.

And so on this Mother's Day, let's thank mothers for all they do to nurture a new generation of men and women of moral character.

Ascension

You've heard people say, "Once you have the right information, you can easily make the right decision." This can be said about life. If we grasp the true purpose of life, we can pursue that purpose.

During these forty-some days, we have been celebrating the paschal or Passover mystery of Jesus Christ, a mystery that includes not only his death and resurrection but also his ascension or return to his Father in glory and the descent of the Spirit of God on the disciples at Pentecost.

The death, resurrection, ascension, and descent are all different aspects of the passage of Jesus from his earthy life through death into a new, indescribable, transformed, heavenly reality—and this reality anticipates our own future.

The ascension we celebrate today is Jesus's final leave-taking from the community of disciples. Jesus had been appearing suddenly from somewhere and then disappearing to somewhere else. The fact is, Jesus has been appearing in glory. That's why he is so different. Jesus took his final leave in the ascension so something new could happen: the descent of the Spirit of God on Pentecost. Yes, the living Christ continues among us, ever active through the Spirit of God.

The author of the book of Acts flat-out indicates that the Lukan Gospel and the Acts of the Apostles are a two-volume work. The Gospel is about Jesus; the Acts is about early Christianity.

The ascension connects Luke and Acts. It signals the close of Jesus's earthly ministry and heralds the beginning of the church's ministry—the proclamation of the good news that Jesus is alive—"to the ends of the earth." (Acts 1:8)

In his letter to the Christian community at Ephesus, Paul prayed that we would grow in wisdom and enlightenment so we would see more clearly God's saving work in Jesus Christ. Jesus is indeed the "head" of the "body," the church, the people of God. And we with our many talents are called to build up this "body of Christ," the mystical body of Christ.

And in the Gospel according to Mark, Jesus told the disciples to be missionary disciples, to proclaim the gospel to every creature. They were now the "hands and feet and eyes and ears and voice" of the living Christ until he comes again in glory at the End Times to transform this universe into a new, indescribable reality. The living Christ has created new relationships for us—with God and with one another. And in light of this fact, I would like to pose three questions:

What make us feel alive? What does it mean to be alive in this new relationship with the living Christ? How really alive in Christ are we?

First, what makes you feel alive? Gazing up at the sky? Experiencing the awesomeness of Niagara Falls or the Grand Canyon? Watching a space shuttle lift off? Watching your favorite team win an exciting game? Hearing Tony Bennett or Carrie Underwood sing? Holding a baby in your arms? Accomplishing a challenging task at work? Any of these experiences, and many more, can make us feel alive.

Pablo Casals, the great twentieth-century cellist and conductor, experienced painful arthritis and severe emphysema at age ninety. Each morning began with agony. Casals would shuffle, badly stooped. But when he sat to play Bach or Brahms, his body slowly came alive with music. Afterward, he would walk with no trace of a shuffle, eat heartily, talk animatedly, and then walk on the beach. He felt alive. Music energized Casals. What energizes you?

My second question is, what does it mean to be alive in Christ? We have been gifted with God's triune life in baptism, our initiation into a community of disciples. In early Christianity, candidates for baptism were often immersed in a pool of water. And water symbolizes life and death. Water can be life-giving or death-threatening if it's a hurricane. And when the candidate stepped down into the pool of water and came up on the other side, it symbolized a dying to self-centeredness and a rising to new life: an others-centered life.

The rite of baptism makes us alive in Christ. To understand the significance, we have to appreciate who we are in relation to God. At birth we lack God's triune life. That's what original sin means: a lack of a relationship. The book of Genesis captures this very graphically. In the beginning, man and woman walked with God and had a friendship with God and one another. Somehow or other, they lost that friendship, and they fell from grace. Genesis describes simply yet powerfully that they "hid" from God; man blamed woman, and even the earthly elements worked against them.

And that is why God became flesh in Jesus of Nazareth. Through the crucified and risen Christ, God reestablished that friendship again and reconnected us to the living Christ. And through the waters of baptism, we enter into this community of disciples, this fellowship of grace. We are alive in Christ.

And the third question is, how really alive in Christ are we? The Spirit of God is within us to bring about the design of God on this planet of ours. That Spirit calls us to continue the saving work of Jesus Christ until he comes again in glory. We are indeed his hands and feet and eyes and ears and voice. And the Spirit of God empowers us to be channels or instruments of faith, hope, love; channels of forgiveness, compassion, truth, and fairness; yes, channels of hospitality, fidelity, responsibility, and self-discipline in our families, workplaces, and communities.

At this time of year, many of us read or hear about commencement speeches. The best advice I ever heard was a brief passage in a commencement speech, and it's this: Twenty-five years or fifty years from now—at home or at work, in the public of your community or in the quiet of some private place—the quality of your life and your soul's destiny will be measured by your character: going the extra mile to help someone in need, helping a child realize his or her potential, being faithful in your relationships and responsibilities, working for the common good, and trusting always in a good and compassionate God who is ever near to us and will guide us safely home.

If we follow that advice, we indeed will be continuing the saving work of Jesus Christ until he comes in glory at the End Times.

Pentecost

I had a Pentecost experience in my office when suddenly a violent storm broke out: torrential rains, thunder clapping, bolts of lightning, high winds, and hailstones.

The lights went out, the computer went off, lightning snapped a tree in two, and another bolt hit a fuse box. And I was standing at the window, watching all this in wonder.

Now you may be thinking, *That's not very smart, standing at the window.*

Anyway, in the midst of this torrential rainstorm, I thought of the biblical story of Noah and the ark, and I pondered whether there was anything I could learn from that story. And there are a few lessons:

1. Plan ahead. When Noah built the ark, it wasn't raining.
2. Stay fit. You may have to do something big.
3. Don't miss the boat.
4. Speed isn't always an advantage. On the ark, snails were on board with cheetahs.
5. The ark was built by amateurs; the *Titanic* was made by professionals.
6. No matter how severe the storm, with God there's a rainbow waiting.

Today we celebrate Pentecost, the outpouring of the Spirit on the disciples centuries ago. Pentecost concludes the Easter season and begins the mission of the church, yours and mine, to continue the work of Jesus Christ until he comes again in triumph at the End Times.

You and I can continue that work by embodying the gifts of the Spirit in our daily lives: true wisdom, compassionate understanding, right judgment, courage, knowledge, reverence, and wonder and awe.

The word *Pentecost* comes from a Greek word meaning "fiftieth," the fiftieth day after Passover. The Hebrews initially celebrated it after harvesting the spring wheat in their fields. Later they associated this festival with the covenant God made with their forebears on Mount Sinai centuries before—a covenant summed up very simply and yet very powerfully in that simple phrase "You are my people and I am your God."

In the Christian tradition, Pentecost celebrates an aspect of the entire paschal mystery, which includes the death, resurrection, and ascension of Jesus Christ—not to mention the descent of the Spirit on the disciples.

The book of Acts describes how the Jews had come to Jerusalem to celebrate Pentecost. And suddenly the Spirit—described in images of wind and fire (images that symbolize power, force, energy, and vitality)—was poured out on the disciples and emboldened them to proclaim the gospel courageously not only to the people in Jerusalem but also eventually to people all around the Mediterranean.

The word of God asks you and me, do we have the courage to stand up, as much as we can, for what is true, right, and good? I always remember that great philosophical quote: "If not you, who; if not now, when?"

The letter of Paul to the Christian community at Corinth in Greece speaks about all the different gifts the Spirit bestows on us—all for the greater common good. In this age of individualism, where we often overemphasize the individual at the expense of the greater common good, Paul's words are a powerful reminder.

People working together can perform extraordinary deeds. Together, we can spark each other's imagination and creativity; together we can encourage and motivate one another, magnify each other's efforts and abilities. And working together, we can accomplish so much more.

For example, each time I enter an airplane, I think about the hundreds of people who take care of it: pilots and flight attendants, schedulers, weather staff, cleaning people, mechanics, marketers, dispatchers, controllers watching radar screens, FAA inspectors ensuring safety, the manufacturers tracking the quality of the planes they built, and many other people.

An airplane requires teamwork. And so, too, does a community, yes, even a faith community. That's Paul's point.

And in the Gospel according to John, the author described a postresurrection appearance of Jesus, in which he breathed on the disciples (as God breathed life into man in the second chapter of Genesis), and in that gesture he bestowed the Spirit on the disciples.

There are many images of the Spirit in the scriptures: fire, wind, force, energy, and power. A classic film captures an image of the Spirit. You may have seen *Chariots of Fire*, a title that stems from a poem by William Blake. The film is about two British runners, Harold Abrahams and Eric Liddell, who won the 1924 Olympics through character, discipline, and courage.

There is a powerful line in the film. Eric Liddell says, "God has made me fast." He can glorify God with his legs and lungs just as we can glorify God with the gifts God has bestowed on us. And then Eric explains, "The power is within."

In a sense, we, too, can become chariots of fire, for this image suggests a power already within us: force and heat, speed and grace, something overpowering. The Spirit of God is within us, bringing about God's plan despite all the obstacles we place in his way.

Yes, the Spirit of God is within us. God is close to us. But how? To begin with, God fashioned the universe, and in so doing, he mirrored his image in earth, sea, sky, and people.

God came closer when he became flesh in Jesus of Nazareth and when he became one of us—he ate and slept, worked and loved, walked and ran, laughed and wept, and lived and died in our midst. This is the great mystery of the incarnation: the Word became flesh.

God came still closer when he wanted to stay with us and yet had to leave us when he gave himself to us in the signs of bread and wine. "This is my body.. my blood." (Luke 22:19-20) Yes, Jesus left, yet he stays with us.

But perhaps God knew that all this wouldn't be quite enough. So before he died, he said to his disciples, "I will ask the Father, and he will

give you another Advocate to be with you always, the Spirit of truth…
it remains with you, and will be in you." (John 14:16-17)

We need not search for God in the universe; we need not envy the
disciples who walked with Jesus. God is in us. Saint Paul wrote, "We are
living temples of God." *This is the great lesson of Pentecost.*

And what does the Spirit of God do within us? This is a tremendous
reality of our faith. The God of the universe, the triune God, lives within
us; we are new creatures, and we have a destiny: eternal life with God.
And that life has already begun in us.

To see what the Spirit of God can do, look at the disciples, whom
God transformed into heroes.

The same Spirit of God who spoke through the prophets, the same
Spirit who overshadowed the Virgin Mary, who descended on the disciples
and lives within the church, made up of saints and sinners, guides human
history—despite its never-ending crises—toward its ultimate fulfillment.
That Spirit lives within you and me and can transform us.

Let us pray today on this feast of Pentecost that we will become
chariots of fire and that the Spirit will empower us to practice the
fruits of the Holy Spirit: love, joy, peace, patience, kindness, generosity,
gentleness, faithfulness, and self-discipline.

The Most Holy Trinity

I begin with a story about a youngster who wanted to meet God. He imagined it was a long trip, so he packed two cans of chips and two sodas, and started walking.

After about three blocks, he met an old man sitting in the park. The boy sat down and opened his book bag. He noticed that the old man looked hungry, so he offered him some chips.

The old man gratefully accepted and smiled at him so beautifully that the boy offered him a soda. Again, the old man smiled. The boy was delighted. They sat there all afternoon, eating and smiling.

Finally, the boy got up to leave, took a few steps, turned around, ran back to the old man, and gave him a hug. The old man gave him his biggest smile ever.

Now when the boy went home, his mother noticed his joy. She asked, "What did you do today that made you so happy?"

He replied, "I had lunch with God."

Meanwhile, the old man returned to his home. His son was stunned by the look of peace and happiness on his father's face and asked, "Dad, what did you do today?"

He replied, "I ate Pringles in the park with God."

The point is this: Too often we underestimate the power of a smile, a kind word, a listening ear, a genuine compliment, an act of caring, all of which have the potential to turn a life around. People come into our lives for a reason, a season, or a lifetime. We can show people the face of God.

Today we celebrate the mystery of the triune God, the fundamental and distinctive truth of Christianity: one God in three. This is a God completely beyond us and yet completely within us.

To put this mystery simply, the God of this universe, a God of wonder and awe, became flesh in Jesus of Nazareth (the mystery of the incarnation) and lives in our midst by the power of the Spirit. Yes, one God in three distinct modes: Father, Son, and Spirit. And so we begin every prayer in the name of the Father, Son, and Holy Spirit.

Now when you hear the name God, what do you immediately think of? The scriptures give us many splendid images of God: God as a walking companion, God who is as tender as a mother. " Can a mother forget her infant…Even should she forget, I will never forget you. '" (Isaiah 49:15) These scriptures also speak of a God who wants to share true wisdom with us.

The image of God in the parables of the Good Shepherd and the prodigal son is balanced with the image in the parable of the last judgment. Yes, there are many splendid biblical images, but all these images fail to fully capture the inexhaustible reality of God. The word of God takes us back to Moses, who posed a series of rhetorical questions about God to his fellow Hebrews in the wilderness, in what we know today as Jordan.

God, Moses said, has appeared to the Hebrews as a Creator, a worker of signs and wonders, and a loving parent. And this God promises peace and prosperity if the Hebrews will be faithful to the covenant God made with them. We might ask ourselves, "How faithful are we to our baptismal promises?"

In his letter to the Romans, Paul spoke about our new relationship with God through Jesus Christ by the power of the Spirit: we are sons and daughters of God and heirs to the kingdom of God. Paul might have asked you and me, "Do we try our best to live in light of our ultimate purpose: heirs to the kingdom of God?" And in the Gospel according to Matthew, Jesus sent us forth by the power of the Spirit to continue his saving work: "In the name of the Father and of the Son and of the holy Spirit." (Matthew 28:19)

The mystery of the triune God, a God utterly beyond us and yet utterly within us, a God who is one as well as diverse, a God of distinctive relationships, invites us to ask ourselves, what kind of a relationship do we have with God?

Most people have a relationship with God, but perhaps it is more subconscious than conscious. We are forever trying to find answers to fundamental questions of human life that people often ask in moments of crisis—for example, the death of a close relative, a life-threatening illness, a broken marriage, the loss of a job or savings, or misunderstandings in family life. In moments such as these, people often ask the most fundamental questions. Does my life have meaning? What is my purpose? Where is my life going? Does anyone really care? These are religious questions.

As we grow older, we may begin to wonder about our lives. We appear to have accomplished so little, and now it is almost over. What was my life all about?

Moreover, life seems to be filled with so many senseless tragedies—murders in our streets, mindless violence in our world, and natural disasters like earthquakes in Nepal or drowning refugees.

But we also have the occasional experiences that shake us into awe and wonder. It could be experiencing a spectacular landmark. Perhaps it's a glorious sunset, the joy of a friendship, or the accomplishment of a goal. Such experiences can lift us out of ourselves into the presence of a power beyond us. We begin to experience the transcendent dimension of our lives.

"Yes," we say, "there must be an awesome power beyond us, a purposeful, gracious, and compassionate God, who is responsible not only for this incredible universe of ours but also for our own very lives."

Catholic Christianity says this power is indeed a gracious and compassionate God who can heal the brokenness of human existence. This God became flesh in Jesus of Nazareth, crucified, risen, and alive in our midst by the power of the Spirit. And that is indeed the mystery of the triune God, a God who is one in three: Father, Son, and Spirit.

The triune God empowers us to continue the saving work of Jesus, to reach out to others with compassion, forgiveness, a smile, a kind word, or a helping hand. And in reaching out, God empowers us to reach up to God.

And just as God showed us his face in Jesus of Nazareth, crucified, risen, and alive by the power of the Spirit, God asks us to show the face of God to one another with a smile, a kind word, a compliment, and a helping hand.

Some of you may have seen the play *Godspell*. It appears over and over again. I love that prayer in *Godspell*: "Three things I pray: to see Thee more clearly; to love Thee more dearly, and follow Thee more nearly, day by day."

Let us pray on this feast of the Trinity and day by day that we might

1. see our triune God more clearly;
2. love God more dearly; and
3. follow God more nearly.

Corpus Christi

I read a review in the Sunday *New York Times* about "The Theology of Atheism" (definitely an oxymoron). And that article brought back memories of a story about an atheist who was walking alongside the river when he suddenly saw a seven-foot grizzly bear charging toward him. He ran as fast as he could, but the bear began to close in on him. Then the fellow tripped and fell, and the bear was right on top of him.

At that instant the fellow, an atheist, cried out, "Oh my God!"

The bear froze. The woods went silent. A bright light shone upon the man, and a voice came out of the sky. "You denied my existence for so many years. Do you expect me to help you out of this predicament?"

The atheist looked directly into the light and said, "It would be hypocritical of me to suddenly ask you to treat me as a believer, but perhaps you could make the *bear* a believer, a Catholic."

"Very well," said the voice. And the bear brought both paws together, bowed its head, and said, "Lord, bless this food, which I am about to receive from thy bounty through Christ our Lord, amen." The moral of the story: be careful what you pray for.

Today we celebrate the feast of the body and blood of Jesus Christ, the Eucharist, also known in Latin as *Corpus Christi*, and so I invite all of us to reflect on the significance of this feast day.

Now there have been many impressive meals in the course of human history, from the very simple to the highly elaborate. There was the first supper, so the book of Genesis says, where the entrée was forbidden fruit. That meal turned into a catastrophe. And there are those endless state banquets where heads of state toast each other over rack of lamb and cherries jubilee.

And then there's the Passover, the seder service, a remembrance of the Jews' deliverance from oppression in Ancient Egypt. The meal table often is the center of family life. Memorable things often take place around meal tables. Families celebrate important transitions in life—birthdays, marriages, graduations, and retirements—around a table.

Sometimes families even argue at meal tables. But an argument can be a positive sign that we care enough to disagree. We agree to disagree. And even if we argue around a table now and then, we share plenty of memorable things there too.

Yes, the meal table is indeed for many the center of family life. And in our global Christian family, the altar or table of the Lord is the center of our faith community. Think about that. We gather around the table of the Lord to celebrate the Lord's Supper, to reenact the mystery of the dying and rising of Jesus Christ so we can re-experience our salvation and nurture the life of God within us.

The word of God proclaimed today takes us back in our imaginations to the Exodus or liberation of the Hebrews from their oppressors in Ancient Egypt. And then in the wilderness, Moses experienced God in the imagery of thunder and lightning, and mediated a covenant in a so-called blood ritual, which symbolized that God and the Hebrews shared the same divine life. Blood symbolizes life, and in this instance, God's life is ours. We, too, carry within our fragile selves God's life. But are we faithful to our covenantal or baptismal promises?

The author of the letter to the Hebrews compared the animal sacrifices in the temple in Jerusalem to the bodily sacrifice of Jesus on the cross. Through his horrifying death and life-giving resurrection, Jesus has opened up to us life beyond this earthly life. Do we live in light of our ultimate purpose? Life eternal with God. And in the Gospel according to Mark, the author recalled the last supper or Passover of Jesus in the upper room in Jerusalem.

When Jesus sat down to that supper, he faced three challenges: First, he had to leave us, and yet he wanted to stay with us. How did he solve this challenge? Listen to his words: "This is my body; this is my blood." The bread and wine look and feel and taste like bread and wine, but they are not. The bread and wine become sacramentally the living Christ, his presence among us until he comes in glory at the End Times.

The second challenge: he wanted to die for each one of us, and yet he could die only once as a human being. How did he solve this challenge? Listen to his words: "Do this in remembrance of me." The same victim who died once for us outside the walls of Jerusalem centuries ago returns to this sacrificial meal today and every day.

The third challenge: he wanted to be one with us, and yet this was impossible this side of heaven. How did he solve this challenge? Listen to his words: "Take and eat; take and drink." Jesus invited us to become one with himself ever so briefly in Communion.

Yes, Jesus had to leave us, and yet he stays with us: the bread and wine become sacramentally the living Christ. Jesus could die but once as a human being.

And so the victim (the lamb, the sacrifice) returns to us today and every day in this sacrificial meal. He wanted to be one with us, and yet he couldn't do so this side of heaven; so he gave us Communion.

But what is the purpose of the bread we eat? The blood we drink? To form us into a vibrant faith community. Paul wrote, "Because the loaf of bread is one, we, though many, are one body, for we all partake of the one loaf." (1 Cor. 10:17)

And this bread we eat and this blood we drink should not only form us into a more vibrant faith community but also empower us to reach out compassionately (especially with our time and talent) to people, especially the people immediately around us. And I emphasize the people immediately around us.

Many of you know about Giacomo Puccini, who wrote such operas as *La Boheme, Madame Butterfly, Tosca,* and *Turandot.* Puccini discovered he had cancer while writing *Turandot.* He began a race against death to complete this opera. He confided in his friend, the conductor Arturo Toscanini, saying, "Who will finish?" Eventually death won; Puccini died in 1924 before he finished the opera.

For the world premiere performance of *Turandot* at Teatro alla Scala in Milan, Toscanini paid respect to Puccini in his own way. He conducted magnificently all the way up to where the master, Puccini, had left off. And then Toscanini stopped and cried out, "Thus far the master wrote."

Others completed the opera, a fact that reminds me of the paraphrase of an old hymn. Christ has no hands but our hands to do His work today.

Christ, the master, calls us to be God centered, other centered. And so we pray that God may reenergize all of us through this Eucharist to be ever more visibly the hands, feet, and voice and ears of Jesus in our everyday lives.

Eleventh Sunday in Ordinary Time

You heard the Bible quotation "There is an appointed time for everything...a time to be silent, and a time to speak." (Eccl. 3: 1-7) Let me illustrate this.

A police officer pulled over a couple for speeding. The husband told the officer, "I had the car on cruise control at sixty."

The wife chimed in. "Sweetheart, you know the car doesn't have cruise control."

The husband turned to his wife and said, "Would you please let me speak?"

The officer then noted, "You're not wearing your seat belt. That's an automatic fine."

The husband explained, "I had it on but took it off when you pulled me over so I could get my license."

To which the wife replied, "Sweetheart, you never wear your seat belt."

As the policeman wrote a second ticket, the husband yelled at his wife, "Let me handle this!"

The officer looked at the wife and asked, "Does he always shout at you?"

She replied, "Only when he's drinking."

There's definitely a time to be silent and a time to speak.

The word of God takes us back in our imaginations to the sixth century before Jesus. Ezekiel saw the collapse of the kingdom of the

South. Babylonia conquered the capital city of Jerusalem, destroyed the temple, and deported many Hebrews.

Yet in the midst of this national trauma, Ezekiel prophesied through this "Thus says the Lord" oracle that God would raise up a tender shoot, a majestic cedar tree, a leader, a Messiah who would bring blessings on the Hebrews. Ezekiel challenged us to hope in God in the midst of despair.

When we're depressed—"down on our luck," so to speak—Ezekiel inspired us to hope in the future. Try to do the right thing every day; try to do the best we can. Stop looking, so to speak, into the rearview mirror and keep looking forward.

In his letter to the Christian community in Corinth, Paul urged us to be courageous and stand up for what is right, true, and good. He challenged us to "please God" and "walk by faith." And remember, he wrote, that we are accountable to God for how we live and behave. There's an old gospel song that sums up today's passage well: This world is not my home, I'm just a-passin' through.

That gospel song gives us plenty to think about. I once read a headstone in an old cemetery. It went like this: "Remember, you who pass by this stone; as you are now, so once was I; and as I am, so you will be; prepare yourself to follow me." And someone had scribbled below that inscription, "To follow you is not my intent, unless I know which way you went." Now there's something to think about as we visit a cemetery.

In the Gospel according to Mark, Jesus spoke about the kingdom of God through a story, a parable. Jesus said the kingdom of God was like a seed you plant, the tiniest of seeds, and what you get is a plant, bigger and better than you ever expected.

The kingdom of God, in other words, is more than what we expect, impossible for us to completely imagine, and better than our wildest dreams. Heaven is the unimaginable come to life.

Today I would like to reflect on Paul's letter, which challenges us to be courageous, to stand for something and not fall for anything. Yes, Paul admonished us to "please God." In other words, make sure we have our priorities straight. Seek first the kingdom of God.

Leo Tolstoy, the celebrated nineteenth-century Russian novelist, philosopher, and reformer, noted that there are only two important questions in life. What shall we do, and how shall we live?

Yes, how shall we live? How shall we please God? Saint Paul would likely have advised us, "By being men and women of moral character."

Let me begin by saying there's a difference between personality and character. Our personality on the surface puts us in a category—for example, cheerful, moody, excitable, and so forth. Character, by contrast, is singular and defines who we are at the core of our innermost selves.

Personality is emotional. Character is ethical. Personality is neither good nor bad. Character, by definition, is either good or bad. By character, one stands out from the crowd. That takes courage.

Few of us will be called to the heights of courage involved in, say, rescuing a human being from a life-threatening situation. However, there is another everyday level of courage, to which all of us are called. It manifests itself in the choices each of us must make about the fundamental values or virtues by which we live. As one author put it, "If we have the courage to discover meaning in life through what we experience, for example, family and friends, and through what we do, for example, a profession, if we see ourselves and others as blessed briefly with earthly life and promised eternal life, if we are true to our inner best selves, we indeed will be able to overcome those moments of anxiety that sneak up on us from time to time." Ours then will truly be a wonderful life.

A person of moral character will choose fair-mindedness over bigotry; the dignity of the person over impersonal business or material advantage; a respect for human beings over the lust for pleasure, power, or personal success; and a willingness to go the extra mile to make something "just right" because it's the better thing to do.

A person of character will have the courage to speak up for what is right and defend what is fair, and he or she won't falter or remain silent out of cowardice and let the crowd take over. But he or she will take a stand on principle and conscience—yes, an informed conscience, even if it is to one's worldly disadvantage, even if others turn against him or her. A person of character will show courage and not simply "get along by going along."

A person of character, in short, will try to choose what is true, good, and right in all decisions, small and great, that affect family, work, career, and social life, the raising of children, relationships with others, even leisure time. They will stand for something.

Paul pleads with us today to be men and women of courage, to "walk by faith," and to please God by the way in which we live and behave. Especially in light of his message to the Corinthians today, all of us are called to seek not what is "fashionable," not what is expected by others, but simply what is right, true, and good. And having found what is right and true and good, as the advertisement says, have the courage to "just do it."

I conclude with a few guideposts as all of us make our earthly pilgrimage toward our heavenly home.

The greatest joy .... Giving

The most satisfying work .... Helping Others

The greatest shot in the arm .... Encouragement

The greatest asset .... Faith in God

The most prized possession .... Integrity

The most powerful channel of communication ... Prayer

Twelfth Sunday in Ordinary Time

How many of you can remember something humorous about your own dad? I can.

My father was always shopping for a bargain. When we were youngsters, he took my two older brothers and me shopping for our Easter or Christmas suits. And with the three of us in tow, he said to the salesman, "I want to see the cheapest suit in the store?"

The salesman looked him in the eye and said, "You're wearing it."

The word *father* or *dad* evokes all kinds of images. And I think of certain qualities my father possessed in abundance (qualities all good fathers possess): love (he tried to do his best for us), commitment (he stuck by us), support (he gave us as much as he could), forgiveness (he wasn't afraid to say he was sorry), communication (he was ready to listen to us), and spirituality (we went to church and prayed together). We spent time together, and he had a good sense of humor.

Here's a touching story. At the Baseball Hall of Fame in Cooperstown, New York, someone found a photo in a crevice under a display case. A man in the photo was wearing a baseball uniform. And stapled to the photo was a note. "You were never too tired to play baseball. On your days off, you helped our little league. You always came to watch me play. You belong in the Hall of Fame, dad. And I only wish you could share this moment with me. Your son, Peter." A son had found a way to put his dad in the Hall of Fame.

Now in the word of God, the book of Job addresses the eternal question. Why do the wicked prosper and the innocent suffer? God doesn't answer the question. He simply used the image of the mighty waters of the sea and its incredible power to say he is mightier than even these waters. Yes, God is the Creator and guide of this awesome universe, and we are simply fragile creatures. God is always in control; we're definitely not.

The author may have asked us to examine our own lives. We live ever so briefly on a planet that is billions of years old. We see astonishing courage and compassion, and also appalling cruelty and injustice. We search for meaning and connectedness. We age, and then we die. Do we know the purpose of our lives?

In his letter to the Christian community in Corinth, Paul spoke about God's saving work. Jesus through his death and resurrection has begun a new era; a new order is emerging. We are new creatures by the grace-filled waters of baptism, destined for life eternal. Paul may be asking us whether we live as new creatures.

And in the Gospel according to Mark, Jesus was on a small boat in the middle of the Sea of Galilee. And suddenly a storm arose with howling winds and crashing waves. How could Jesus be asleep? But he was. The frightened disciples woke Jesus to cry out for deliverance, for salvation. Jesus simply calmed the waters and asked the frightened disciples, "Do you not yet have faith in God?"

One of my favorite college books was *Man's Search for Meaning* by Viktor Frankl. In the 1930s, Frankl had a wife, two children, a good profession as a psychiatrist, and a comfortable home. But he lost all of these, every earthly thing he treasured; first, he lost his home and profession. Then, in the Nazi death camp at Dachau, he lost his wife and children.

These losses brought him face-to-face with the fundamental questions of human life: Who really am I? How should I live? What is the purpose of my life?

Frankl discovered that people could put up with incredible hardships, cruelties, and sufferings without losing their will to live and their respect for others if they saw that these hardships had some greater meaning.

In their hearts, people yearn for something or someone beyond themselves who can give greater meaning and value to their lives. And this can take different forms, such as family, a profession, a passion for justice, the greater common good, and so forth. When people find something that gives transcendent meaning to their lives, that purpose awakens new energies within them. They see more and live better; in short, they become men and women of faith.

To be human is to live by faith. We are by nature believers. Think about the ordinary things we do. We turn on the car; we don't expect it to blow up. We sit in the church pew; we don't expect it to collapse.

Our faith is a gift from God that empowers us to relate to the triune God as our Creator, redeemer, and sanctifier. Faith is richer and deeper than belief. Our Catholic faith calls us to commit ourselves to Jesus Christ, to follow him who is our way to eternal life, our truth who sets us free from falsehoods, and our Light who illuminates the darkness around us as we journey toward our heavenly home. Faith is about connectedness to a person, Jesus Christ. It's relational.

Belief is a profession of the essential truths of our Catholic faith that we proclaim every Sunday, for example, in the fourth-century Nicene Creed. We say, "I believe in one God" despite the many today who question the existence of God, perhaps in the face of overwhelming evil.

We say our God is "almighty, maker of heaven and earth, of all things visible and invisible." We profess there is Someone completely Other and beyond ourselves; One who sustains and guides to an ultimate purpose everything that is.

And yes, we believe in "one lord, Jesus Christ. He came down from heaven." Why? To heal our brokenness, to invite us into his triune life forever. Yes, something isn't quite right with this planet. There is love, life, courage, integrity, and compassion, but there is also cruelty, greed, hate, ignorance, lies, and violations.

This planet cries out for a healer, a reconciler. And Jesus, who for our sake was crucified, died, was buried, and rose again, is our healer, our reconciler; and his resurrection anticipates our own indescribable life beyond this earthly life.

We believe in "the Holy Spirit, the Lord, the giver of life."

The power of the Spirit is within us and empowers us to pursue our true destiny—eternal life with the triune God and one another—and to do good for others.

And we believe in "one, holy, catholic and apostolic" community of disciples. We acknowledge "one baptism" and look toward "the resurrection of the dead and the life of the world to come."

This creed underscores the essential beliefs of our faith, and what we believe truly matters. May our faith be the binoculars, so to speak, through which we see what lies beneath and beyond immediate appearances: the reality and presence of God all around us, within us, and in one another, a presence that sustains and guides this universe of ours.

Pope Saint John Paul II advised the United Nations assembly: "It is no accident that we are here. Each and every human person has been created in the 'image and likeness' of the One who is the origin of all that is. We have within us the capacities for wisdom and virtue. With these gifts and with the help of God's grace, we, a faith-filled people, can build…a civilization worthy of the human person."

Thirteenth Sunday in Ordinary Time

In summer, many of us think we need a vacation. How many think they need a vacation? I do. But then I saw some mathematics that questioned whether I should even take one day off. And here are the numbers.

There are 365 days in the year (except leap year with 366 days). But we take weekends off, so subtract 104 days. That leaves 261 workdays. But we ordinarily work eight hours a day. We're doing something else the other sixteen hours. And so subtract another 174 days. That leaves 87 working days.

But wait! We eat lunch every day, and although lunch hours vary, the average person probably consumes forty-five days per year at lunch. That leaves forty-two working days. And coffee breaks? Figure twenty-one days over the course of the year. That leaves twenty-one days to get our work done. From those twenty-one days, subtract at least a two-week vacation—ten workdays. That leaves us only eleven actual full workdays in the entire year.

And many companies now allow ten paid holidays per year. After subtracting the ten paid holidays from the eleven days remaining, we've got one full workday to our credit, and I want to take a vacation. An employer may say, "Forget it!" Somehow or other these calculations just don't sound right, so I'm going to take a vacation in July, and I hope you do too.

The word of God, just proclaimed, takes us back to the first century before Jesus, to the wisdom literature of ancient Israel, a collection of books about how to live and behave. The author reflected on the theme of life and death, mortality or perishability, and immortality or imperishability.

The author clearly told us that God created us in his own image and likeness; we possess the spark of the divine within ourselves. We are destined for a relationship with God and one another forever. But do we live in light of this purpose?

Paul in his letter urged the Christian community of Corinth in Greece to be generous in a collection for the poor Christians in Jerusalem. And why should the community do such a gracious act? Paul wrote that Jesus Christ himself was an example of generosity par excellence. The eternal Word became materially poor in Jesus so we could become spiritually rich.

In the Gospel according to Mark, we are inspired by the faith of two people in the power of Jesus. One is a woman who had been ill for twelve years and spent all her money on doctors, to no avail. She got sicker and sicker. In fear and trembling, but with extraordinary faith, she touched the cloak of Jesus and was healed. The power of touch—think about it. With a touch, we tell people, "I love you; I'm so sorry. I don't know what to say."

Jesus touches us especially in the sacraments—water, oil, bread, and wine; and in that touch his grace—his life—goes out to us as it did to the anonymous woman in this Gospel. Yes, in touching the living Christ sacramentally, we are touched with God's grace, God's life. And when we touch others in need, we give life—love, understanding, sympathy—to someone in need. Yes, this is the power of touch.

In another example, a Jewish official named Jairus begged Jesus to heal his dying daughter. And Jesus took the little girl by the hand and healed her. Again, here is the power of touch.

In these two people, we witness the mixture of the power of faith, the power of touch, and the power of prayer. Today I would like to reflect briefly on prayer and its power, a key ingredient in our lives of faith.

One spiritual writer compared the stages of prayer to the seven ages of man in Shakespeare. At twenty we pray we will wake up romantic. At thirty we pray we will wake up married. At forty we pray we will wake up successful. At seventy we pray we will wake up healthy, and at eighty we pray we will wake up.

So, then, what is prayer? Whether we know it or not, we are already in the presence of God. Prayer simply brings to consciousness the presence of God within us. To pray is to make ourselves available to God so that when God comes knocking at the door of our hearts, so to speak, we are ready to invite him into our lives.

Now, there are many methods or pathways or windows into the presence of God. We simply have to find the style of prayer that suits us best. Let me briefly explore some approaches to prayer I think can enrich our relationship and friendship with God.

First are familiar prayers. The Our Father, the stations of the cross, the mysteries of the rosary, the peace prayer of St. Francis—all these, when pondered slowly, can be passageways into the presence of God. Yes, they can enrich our friendship with God. Above all, this Eucharist, the perfect prayer of the church, is the primary pathway into the presence of God. In the Eucharist, we experience by faith the presence of the living Christ sacramentally in the signs of bread and wine.

Second is the prayer of praise. Praise is the bubbling over of the Spirit within us, taking us out of ourselves and into God's presence. Francis of Assisi was always singing praises. Witness the "Canticle of the Sun," whose first words begin the pope's new encyclical or letter on care of our common home, mother earth. Francis of Assisi saw God in brother sun, sister moon, wind and fire and water, and all creatures. Yes, praise recognizes our fundamental relationship: humble creatures vis-à-vis an awesome Creator. A hymn titled "All Creatures of our God and King" makes clear that all creatures are invited to lift their voices in praise to God.

A third form of prayer is taking a passage from scripture and slowly meditating on the meaning of that passage. We all have a favorite scripture passage. Maybe it's "I am the way, the truth and the life" or "Whatever you do to the least of my brothers and sisters, you do for me" or "Come to me, all you who find life burdensome." What's your favorite scripture passage? Slowly reflecting on our favorite readings can bring us into the presence of God.

There are many other forms of prayer. The prayer of silence: without any words or images, we quietly feel the presence of God within us. There is the prayer of petition. Like Christ himself, we shouldn't hesitate to recognize our dependence on God and pray for our daily needs and those of others.

There is the prayer of suffering. Jesus is the model for the prayer of suffering. While racked in fear and pain—in the garden of Gethsemane, on the way to his execution, on the cross itself—he trusted ever more deeply in his Father's love for him. Almost anything we see or experience can be a prayer. Yes, all creatures and all earthly experiences can be pathways or windows into the presence of God, who is all around us.

There's no time like the present. May the examples of faith in today's Gospel—an anonymous woman and a Jewish official—inspire us to nurture our own faith with a key ingredient, daily prayer. And may we feel its power in our daily lives.

Fourteenth Sunday in Ordinary Time

On July 4, 1776, a short but stirring statement was read to the public for the first time outside Independence Hall in Philadelphia. "We hold these truths to be self-evident, that all men are created equal, that they are endowed by their Creator with certain unalienable rights, that among these are Life, Liberty and the pursuit of Happiness."

No American document has had a greater impact on the wider world. As we celebrate the anniversary of the Declaration of Independence, let us give thanks to God for our many blessings.

Philadelphia brings to mind a story about Archbishop Fulton Sheen. He was scheduled to speak at the Philadelphia town hall and decided to walk from his hotel. But he got lost. He asked some teenagers for directions, which they happily gave him. One of them asked, "What are you doing at the town hall?"

Bishop Sheen said, "I'm giving a lecture on how to get to heaven. Do you want to come along?"

The teenager replied, "Are you kidding? You don't even know how to get to the town hall." So much for directions.

The word of God, just proclaimed, takes us back to the sixth century before Jesus (the 500s) to a man by the name of Ezekiel. The sixth century was a catastrophe for the Hebrews. They lost everything they thought would endure forever; ancient Babylonia had conquered their kingdom, abolished their monarchy, set fire to Jerusalem, demolished the temple, and deported many people.

And here the Spirit of God entered into Ezekiel and empowered him to challenge the halfhearted Hebrews, a tough audience, to reform their lives, to reorient themselves to God and one another, and to become other centered and not self-centered.

As I listen to Ezekiel, I think of the things God won't ask us on judgment day:

1. God won't ask what kind of car we drove. He'll ask how many people we gave a lift to.
2. God won't ask about the clothes in our closet. He'll ask how many people we helped to clothe.
3. God won't ask what our job title was. He'll ask whether we worked with integrity.
4. God won't ask how many friends we had. He'll ask how many people we befriended.
5. And finally God won't note the color of our skin. He'll note the content of our character.

Yes, the word of God in Ezekiel challenges us to live an other-centered life: a life with God and a life for others. In his letter to the Christian community in Corinth, Greece, Paul wrote "a thorn in the flesh was given to me." (2 Cor. 12:7) Biblical scholars have debated for centuries about what this disability was that seemed to handicap Paul's ministry. I think of many well-known people in modern times who overcame and transcended their handicaps, including Helen Keller and FDR. Even Beethoven was deaf.

Paul lived a life with and for God, a purpose-driven life. In fact, Paul faced many tough audiences, but he said the power of God's grace was sufficient for him to overcome so many hardships and problems. He was even grateful for this "disability," because Jesus was his model par excellence. Powerless on the cross, Jesus burst forth, all powerful, from the tomb into a new, heavenly reality, a divine life that is ours as well.

And in the Gospel according to Mark, the Spirit of God entered into Jesus and empowered him to speak to a tough audience, his own relatives, and friends in Nazareth. But they rejected his good news. Who is this, the carpenter's son? One of us? And Jesus was amazed at their lack of faith or trust in God.

Ezekiel, Paul, and Jesus all spoke to tough audiences that sometimes were downright hostile. All three must have been disappointed at times when their audiences seemed to turn them and their message off. Yes, they must have felt misunderstood, unappreciated, disheartened, and even depressed at times. And so I would like to focus briefly on depression.

Depression strikes most of us in some form or other at some point in our lives. But how can we deal with depression and make it work for us instead of against us?

First, I'm talking here about occasional, minor, normal depression and not severe, ongoing, debilitating depression. When depression is severe and ongoing, we need professional help at once. But depression is sometimes a temporary occurrence. For no apparent reason, we feel blue, out of sync, and unable to motivate ourselves.

I know of at least three basic forms of depression:

1. One form occurs when our chemical balance is out of whack. Professionals can help us manage this imbalance with medication. And that's why a good physical examination is always helpful in addressing depression.

2. A second form of depression is caused by "something" outside us. It's a loss that affects our well-being—for example, the death of a parent, spouse, or child; a divorce; a retirement; an empty nest (the children are gone); the end of a relationship; or unemployment. Time generally helps heal depression due to loss. Support groups are invaluable in dealing with loss, and there are many available in the community.

3. A third form of depression is often linked with stress. We run out of energy to deal with the demands we think are made on us. For example, a person tries desperately to do everything perfectly, just right. But most things in life don't generally work out that way. Often we have to muddle through a situation and make the best of it. Stressed-out people often take on the expectations of others without expressing their own limitations, without saying no.

How then can we deal positively with depression?

1. As we grow older and wiser, we need to realize that trying to do everything perfectly doesn't matter as much. We may say yes to something but at our pace and in our way. It also becomes easier to say no when we realize our own limitations. Yes, we'll try to do what things we have to do well, but we won't take on more than we can handle.

2. We need to recognize our early stress symptoms so we can deal with them. For example, we know we're getting depressed when we (fill in the blanks) … get irritable, can't sleep. If we're irritable, this mood may be telling us we need to get away briefly from a particular situation. And if we feel unmotivated, this feeling may be telling us to do something more creative and so forth.

3. We need to acknowledge our depression so we can take control of it. How can we give our lives meaning and zest again? Engage in physical activity, such as walking, gardening, and cleaning. Get up out of that chair. Communicate with your family. Let them know how you feel. We can ask them, for example, to be more reasonable if we think they are taking advantage of us. Take charge of your own life. If work has become boring, change your habits and vary your routine. Do something you like, call friends, lend a helping hand, volunteer, find something to look forward to, and rekindle your spiritual life by reading the Bible or watching a religious DVD.

Last but not least, a fellow creature, such as a dog or cat or bird, can be a treasured companion.

So if we're feeling at times the way Ezekiel, Paul, and Jesus must have felt at times—disappointed, misunderstood, underappreciated, or depressed—we should consider these suggestions so we can make the situation work for us, not against us.

Remember especially Saint Paul's words today. "[God's] grace is sufficient for you" whatever comes your way. God is always with us.

May the Lord give you his peace.

Fifteenth Sunday in Ordinary Time

Iheard about a pastor contemplating how he was going to ask his parishioners for additional money to complete roof repairs on the church. Now, the pastor often asked the organist for advice about such matters, but on this particular Sunday the organist was sick, and a substitute was brought in. So the pastor said impatiently to the substitute organist, "You'll have to think of something to play after I announce the bad news that the parish needs twenty thousand dollars more than what's budgeted to complete the roof repairs."

After Communion, the pastor pleaded with the parishioners, "Anyone who can pledge five hundred dollars or more, would you please stand up?"

At that moment, the organist played "The Star Spangled Banner." The parishioners stood, and the pastor completed the repairs and made the substitute the regular organist. Now that's a good fund-raising technique.

Sidney Poitier appeared in over forty films, including such classics as *Raisin in the Sun*. In fact, *Raisin in the Sun* was a Broadway play. In the story line, an African-American family living in a tenement in Chicago in the late 1950s suddenly inherits $10,000 from the father's life insurance policy. The mother wants to use the money as a down payment on a small house. The daughter wants to realize her dream of going to medical school. But the son pleads to use the $10,000 to open a convenience store with a friend. Against her better judgment, the mother agrees to her son's plan. But the so-called friend skips town with the $10,000.

The son can barely bring himself to tell his mother and sister what happened. And when he does, the sister launches into a tirade. But her mother interrupts her and says, "I thought I taught you to love your brother."

"Love him!" the daughter says. "There's nothing left to love!"

But the mother replies, "There is always something left to love. And if you haven't learned that, you haven't learned anything … When do you think it's time to love your brother the most: when he's done something good and made things easy for us? No! Not at all. It's when he's at his lowest and can't believe in himself because the world has whipped him badly. When you start measuring your brother, measure him right. And make sure you've taken into account what hills and valleys he's come through before he got where he is."

The mother had it exactly right. There is always something to love. And the worse things are, the more there is to love. The Jesus of the Gospels assures us of his unconditional love and unconditional forgiveness, especially when things aren't going our way. Jesus asks us to be as ready as he was to lift up one another, to forgive, to support, and to love, especially those who may disappoint us the most or make messes out of their lives and the lives of those closest to them. And that, I think, is what the Jesus of the Gospels asks us to do.

The word of God takes us to the eighth century before Jesus (the 700s), to Israel's divided kingdom of the north, and to a man named Amos. Amos was told to go back home to the kingdom of the South and make a living there as a prophet. Amos said he never wanted to be a prophet, only a sheepherder. But, Amos said, God had called him to prophesy, so prophesy he did about social justice, about fairness, honesty, and compassion in our relationships with one another. Amos may have asked us to examine our relationships with one another.

Paul's letter to the Christian community at Ephesus begins with a prayer about the blessings God bestowed on us through Jesus Christ. Through Christ we have been chosen to become sons and daughters of God and heirs to God's kingdom. Paul challenged us to live holy lives, to reflect the glory or presence of God.

And in the Gospel according to Mark, Jesus sent his disciples out to proclaim the kingdom of God, our destiny beyond this earthly life;

to live simply so others can simply live; to reorient our lives to God; to be hospitable; to become healers; and to recognize our complete dependency on God. Today I would like to take up an overriding theme from the prophet Amos: our relationships with one another.

Jesus connected our love of God to our love for one another. Matthew 25 says this loudly and clearly. When I was hungry, when I was thirsty, you did something. The point is this: We can't say we love God and yet neglect our fellow human beings. Our love for one another doesn't depend on what others can do for us. Who were the beneficiaries of Jesus's love? By and large, they were people who apparently couldn't do much in return.

Jesus made some radical demands on us in regard to our relationships with one another. Carefully read Matthew 5. For example, Jesus said, "Give to everyone who asks." Who can possibly do that, even if you won millions in a lottery? It's not always possible. But that particular demand indicates the thrust or direction of our lives. We need to be generous with what we have, especially with our time, talents, and treasures.

Jesus said elsewhere, "To the person who strikes you on one side of the face, offer the other side as well." That sounds like pacifism. But sometimes we need to stand up against wrongs; we may even have to take someone's life in self-defense. Again, Jesus indicates the thrust or direction of our lives; that is, we should do our best to be peacemakers, healers, bridge builders, reconcilers, forgivers.

Now these radical demands of Jesus, of course, have to be linked to the mission of Jesus. Jesus proclaimed that the kingdom of God is in our midst. Yes, the kingdom is here but not completely or fully here. You and I live in between the historical coming of Jesus in Bethlehem and the final coming of Jesus in glory at the End Times.

And so we live in the tension. Often we fall short of these ethical ideals of Jesus because we have within ourselves a so-called pull or tendency to not always choose the good. We call this tendency "original sin."

But the power of God within us can overcome this pull or tendency, and that power of God enables us to have a good relationship with God and one another. How? By sharing what we have with others and for others. By sharing our time with our families, listening to them. By sharing our talents: a smile or skill that will uplift or help someone else. By sharing our treasure, especially with needy people, if we can.

All of us have the potential to do great things for God. And they begin with small, ordinary things. And so I pray that the word of God will inspire us to do our best to seek a better relationship with God and our fellow human beings.

Sixteenth Sunday in Ordinary Time

July is when many people put on bathing suits, and they want to look good. That may mean a crash diet. Which reminds me of a story about a chat in an Irish pub. "Good news, Nora! My husband is on a diet, and he told me that he is losing four pounds a week. So, if my numbers are correct, I'll be rid of him completely in eighteen months!" That's an interesting way to look at a diet.

The word of God takes us back to the late seventh or early sixth century before Jesus (the late 600s and early 500s), to a so-called prophet of doom and gloom named Jeremiah. Jeremiah lived during a very unstable and chaotic period in the history of ancient Israel. He saw the Hebrews lose everything they thought would endure forever. Babylonia conquered their kingdom, abolished their monarchy, destroyed their capital city of Jerusalem, and executed or deported many Hebrews. Jeremiah blamed the kings of ancient Israel for this catastrophe. The kings, he said, were bad shepherds; they forgot their purpose and repeatedly broke God's covenant. These kings focused only on enriching themselves at the expense of others. They forgot their purpose and ignored the greater common good.

Jeremiah then looked beyond these bad kings to a future shepherd king who would renew God's covenant with his people and seek what was right, true, and fair for all. Jeremiah may have asked us whether we do our best to stand up for what is right, true, and fair, whether we are God centered and not self-centered.

In his letter to the Christian community at Ephesus in Turkey, Paul spoke about the blessings God has bestowed on us through Jesus Christ: friendship with God, peace, and reconciliation. These are virtues so many regions, especially in the Middle East and Africa, desperately cry out for today. Paul may have asked us whether we nurture our friendship with God through regular prayer. Do we try to be peacemakers and reconcilers?

In the Gospel according to Mark, the author portrayed Jesus as the compassionate Good Shepherd who guides us toward our ultimate purpose: eternal life beyond this earthly life. But unfortunately so many people are wandering about aimlessly with little sense of purpose. Jesus said they are leaderless, like sheep without a shepherd.

The theme of leadership—or the lack thereof—weaves in and out of the Jeremiah and Mark passages. In our political arena, we may wonder where the Roosevelts, Lincolns, and Washingtons are.

What is leadership? There is an interesting book titled *Learning to Lead*. The authors write that people today want leaders who have a sense of purpose, generate trust, communicate hope, and can translate vision into results.

Leaders communicate purpose in a way that galvanizes, energizes, and enthralls people. They also generate trust because it is the glue that binds people together and inspires hope. Leaders have a clear vision of the future and are committed to getting there, to bringing along their team. Lastly, it's not enough to have vision unless you have the ability to inspire people to produce results.

Leadership, I believe, begins and ends with self. Leaders are made, not born, and they usually create themselves. They know who they are, what their strengths and weakness are, and how best to emphasize their strengths and compensate for their weaknesses. They know what they want, how they want it, and how to communicate what they want to others so they can galvanize them into action.

Leaders also have the right habits that generally create their destinies. I think Stephen Covey's book *The Eighth Habit* has some good advice for all of us. I cite four of the habits:

1. Be proactive. In other words, take the initiative; be responsible.
2. Begin with the end in mind. Develop a mental image of how you would like your projects, including your own life, to turn out.

3. Put first things first. In other words, use discipline to put off today's pleasures for greater future pleasures.
4. Synergize with people. In other words, the whole is greater than the parts.

Leaders ultimately have a can-do attitude about the challenges of life. But you may say, "That's fine for political leaders but what about religious leaders?"

St. Bonaventure, a great thirteenth-century Franciscan theologian, had something to say about leadership that may resonate with us in the twenty-first century. The primarily role of a religious leader, he wrote, is to give back to God the men and women God gifted to us in our local community. Bonaventure used seven metaphors to describe this primary task; the religious leader is architect, farmer, shepherd, intercessor, doctor, sentinel, and leader.

Let me describe these Bonaventure metaphors briefly. Paul wrote to the Christian community in Corinth, "Like a wise master builder, I laid a foundation." (1 Cor. 3:10) And to the Ephesians, that Christ Jesus himself is "the capstone. Through him the whole structure is held together and grows into a temple sacred in the Lord. In him you also are being built together into a dwelling place of God." (Eph. 2:20-22)

Religious leaders continually have to repair a holy temple that may be spiritually run down or deteriorating. Bonaventure's inspiration was the experience of Francis of Assisi in the Chapel of San Damiano; Francis heard the crucified voice of Jesus say, "Rebuild my House."

This call to rebuild is a challenge in every generation. Religious leaders also must be farmers, cultivating virtues and tilling the field in the spirit of Saint Paul.

Religious leaders have to be shepherds too. Saint Peter, to whom Jesus said, "Feed my sheep," was an example of holiness, of intercessors who stand before God in prayer, pleading the cause of the people before God and the cause of God before the people entrusted to their pastoral care. They are continually in touch with God and people.

Religious leaders are doctors who cleanse and bandage wounds. The scriptures advise, "Is anyone among you sick? He should summon the leaders of the church, and they should pray over him and anoint

[him] with oil in the name of the Lord." (James 5:6) They are sentinels watching out for potential spiritual dangers in the spirit of the prophet Ezekiel: "I have appointed you a sentinel." (Ezek. 33:7) And lastly, they are leaders who protect those entrusted to them; yes, even to the point of ultimate sacrifice—in other words, martyrdom.

An essay by Robert Greenleaf titled "The Servant as Religious Leader" challenges religious leaders to "work to increase the number of religious leaders who are capable of holding their own against the forces of destruction, chaos, and indifference that are always with us." More than ever, we need religious leaders who can pray well, act effectively and responsibly, and include laypeople in leadership in the local community.

Religious leaders must especially inspire people in liturgy, call them to deeper faith, help people meet their needs, and work well with them. Above all, they need to be sacramental: leaders who know God is encountered not only in liturgies but also in the ordinariness of human existence and in the relationships and activities of human life. Let us pray for leaders who can do precisely that.

Seventeenth Sunday in Ordinary Time

I heard the story about a Pat and Mike, who were flying for the first time to Ireland. And in the middle of the flight, the captain announced that one of the four engines had shut down, so the plane would be one hour late into Shannon Airport. About a half hour later, the captain announced that the second engine had shut down and that the plane would be two hours late.

When the captain announced that the third engine had shut down and that the plane would be three hours late, Mike said, "My God. If the fourth engine shuts down, we'll be in the air all night."

So much for first-time flyers.

The word of God, just proclaimed, carries us back in our imaginations to two great ninth-century prophets of ancient Israel, Elijah and his companion and successor, Elisha. These two prophets often railed against Israel's "bad" kings: their injustices, their infidelities to the covenant, and their worship of creaturely things rather than their Creator-God. In fact, Elijah, so the Hebrew tradition goes, was taken up into heaven in a whirlwind, with a fiery chariot and fiery horses, and would reappear just before the long-awaited Messiah.

In today's passage an unknown man brought loaves of bread to Elisha. Why? To be offered to God. Elisha surprisingly directed that these loaves be given to the hungry people, a sign of God's providence. The author may have asked us whether we recognize God's generosity and care for us in our own lives.

Paul wrote from prison to the Christian community in Ephesus, in Turkey, urging them to live a life worthy of their calling as sons and daughters of God. Imitate the attitudes and behaviors of Jesus, he said. Ask from time to time, what would Jesus do in this situation? Paul challenged the Ephesians to practice virtue and to be humble—in other words, to recognize who they were: mere creatures in the presence of an awesome Creator.

Paul continued, advising the community to be forgiving, kind and thoughtful, patient, loving, peacemakers. And remember what binds us together: One Lord, one faith, one baptism.

In the Gospel according to John, Jesus mesmerized the people with signs and wonders. In this passage, the author described the multiplication of loaves and fishes, alluding not only to the Jewish Passover but also to the Eucharist. Notice the words *take*, *bless*, *break*, and *give*. And the people recognized Jesus as the long-awaited prophet who would usher in the messianic age.

The theme of hunger weaves in and out of the Elisha and Gospel stories. So many people today hunger not only for bread but also for justice, freedom, understanding, peace, and yes, God.

In his recent pastoral visit to South America, Pope Francis highlighted these hungers. In fact, Pope Francis continually challenges us to satisfy the different hungers of the human family, to practice the so-called corporal works of mercy.

The most concrete teaching of Jesus about how to treat people can be found in his depiction of the Last Judgment in Matthew 25. Jesus proclaimed that we will be judged by our positive response to the hungry, the thirsty, the stranger, the naked, and the prisoner. In other words, Jesus said that we love God to the extent that we care for our fellow human beings.

How do we care for one another? A blueprint can be found in the so-called seven corporal works of mercy. You know these:

Feed the hungry. Every day millions of people, especially fifty million refugees, according to the United Nations, are hungry. Countless children suffer starvation and malnutrition, and thousands die each day.

Jesus commanded us to feed the hungry. In doing so, we feed Jesus himself. But what can we do? We might contribute to such organizations as Catholic Relief Services. Or, closer to home, we might feed intellectually hungry children or grandchildren by mentoring them in reading or writing skills. Or we might volunteer in religious education to nurture youngsters in their hunger for God. There are countless opportunities to feed the hungry: physically, intellectually, spiritually, and socially.

Give drink to the thirsty. When we pollute the air, when waste makes water undrinkable, we put lives at risk. We have a responsibility to care for this planet of ours, to be good stewards of God's universe, to look after our "garden." Pope Francis, in his latest letter, "Laudato Si," urges us to care for our common home, this planet of ours. Not littering, cleaning, and fixing up can demonstrate that we do care about this planet, our common home.

Clothe the naked. Jesus said we should clothe the naked. In other words, we should do what we can to create a better life for the poor. What about a fall or spring "closet cleaning"? Do we really need all those clothes? Why not donate them?

Shelter the homeless. In cities around the world, the number of homeless people on the streets is increasing. Human beings deserve the dignity and decency that come from having a place to come home to. Yes, government should provide systemic solutions to minimize the causes—for example, meaningful work. But we also can volunteer to work with or support, for example, Habitat for Humanity, which creates homes for needy families.

Visit the sick. Jesus commanded us to visit and comfort them with hope. Yes, their care and dying require better attention. The sick, especially the terminally ill, need our presence. A short visit can do wonders. Our presence allows them to talk about their fears and anxieties, and to transcend feelings of loneliness.

Ransom the captive. Connected to this is the fight for human rights, including political and religious freedom, the right to seek the truth, and the right to economic conditions that foster dignity and to an environment conducive to raising a family. We need to stand up for the right of the unborn to life in this world and the right of the elderly to die with dignity.

Another dimension of this call is concern for people in our prisons. We can visit them to show someone cares, share faith, teach, pray, and give hope.

Finally, bury the dead. Franciscans celebrate every year the transitus (or passing) of Saint Francis of Assisi on October 3. It is a moving celebration about our own pilgrimage from this earth through the mystery of death into eternal life. Mourning someone's passing is natural. We might reach out to mourners, not just at the wake and funeral but through the grieving process, by participating in the bereavement ministry.

With a lively imagination, we can think of 101 ways to practice the so-called corporal works of mercy in our daily lives as Jesus has called us to do. On the day of judgment, our prayer is to hear God say to us, "Come…inherit the kingdom…For I was hungry and you gave me food, I was thirsty and you gave me drink, a stranger and you welcomed me, naked and you clothed me, ill and you cared for me, in prison and you visited me." (Matthew 25:34-36)

Yes, how we live today has profound—indeed eternal—consequences on our tomorrow. Let's do our best to make God's mercy an integral part of our lives.

Eighteenth Sunday in Ordinary Time

You may have heard this story about the Noah of the Bible who now lives in the United States.

God said to Noah, "Build another ark. You have six months before I start the rain."

Six months later, God looked down and saw Noah but no ark. "Noah," God roared, "I'm starting the rain! Where is the ark?"

"Forgive me, Lord," begged Noah, "but things have changed. The building inspector says I need a sprinkler system. And my neighbors claim I violated zoning laws by building the ark in my yard, so I had to go to the board of appeals.

"There's a ban on cutting local trees to save the spotted owl. I tried to convince environmentalists, but no go. And in gathering animals, I was told that I was confining wild animals against their will.

"The trade unions say I can't use my sons. They insist I have to hire union workers with ark-building experience. What's worse, the IRS seized all my assets, claiming I'm trying to leave the country illegally with endangered species. So, forgive me, Lord, but it would take at least ten more years for me to finish this ark."

Suddenly the skies cleared, and the sun began to shine.

Noah looked up in wonder and asked, "You mean you're not going to destroy the world?"

"No," said God. "The government beat me to it."

The word of God takes us back to the thirteenth-century BC exodus or escape of the Hebrews from their oppressors in Egypt. The Hebrews now were in the wilderness—hungry and thirsty and complaining to God. Life with our oppressors in Egypt, they said, was better than life in the wilderness. But God is always faithful to his promises. God miraculously provided food: quail (probably some kind of low-flying migratory birds) and manna (probably a substance from a desert scrub).

This providential wilderness experience was a transformative happening for many Hebrews, who recognized God's incredible care for them. The author may have asked us whether we also recognize God's providential care for us.

In his letter to the Christian community at Ephesus in Turkey, Paul spoke about us as new creatures who must die to the vices of the old self and live the virtues of the new one. The triune God lives within us, Paul wrote elsewhere, and is transforming us into living temples of God's presence. He calls us through the grace-filled waters of baptism to manifest the glory of God. Paul may have asked us whether we manifest the glory or presence of God in our everyday attitudes and behavior.

In the Gospel according to John, the author highlighted one of the seven "I am" sayings of Jesus: "I am the bread of life." (John 6:35) Elsewhere Jesus said, "I am the light of the world; I am the good shepherd; the vine; the resurrection; the way, the truth, the life; the door to heaven." The phrase "I am" alludes to the third chapter in the book of Exodus, where Moses asked God who he was. And God responded, "I am the One who causes to be everything that is." The "I am" sayings allude to Jesus's divinity. Yes, Jesus, the bread of life, came down from heaven to satisfy our deepest hungers.

A remarkable Jewish theologian named Abraham Heschel suffered a near-fatal heart attack a few years before he died. He said to a friend, "When I regained consciousness, my first feeling was not of despair or anger; I felt only gratitude to God for my life. I was ready to depart. Take me, Lord, for I have seen so many miracles in my lifetime."

Heschel wrote, "I did not ask for success in life; I asked for wonder, and God gave it to me." In fact, one of his books is titled *I Asked for Wonder.*

Today's Gospel reflects on God's most splendid gift of wonder, the Eucharist. The word of God alludes to three moments in our salvation history:

- The thirteenth century before Jesus (or the Hebrew Exodus)
- The first century of our Christian era (or Jesus's passage into glory)
- This Eucharistic celebration

Each of these moments is an exodus, a departure, a going out:

- The escape of the Hebrews from Egypt
- Jesus's passage from this earthly life into eternal life (Jesus anticipates our own exodus or passage)
- Our own going out from the Eucharistic celebration to our fellow human beings in community

The word of God references the escape or exodus of the Hebrews from Egypt. It was the wonder of wonders. Their escape is a prototype of our liberation, our deliverance. Jews today in the Passover seder recognize "It is our duty to thank, praise, laud, glorify, exalt, honor, bless, extol, and adore God who wrought all these miracles for our ancestors and ourselves; God brought us forth...from darkness into great light, and from servitude into redemption." (from B. Talmud, Pesachim 116b) Every seder rekindles an expectation that the Messiah will come.

The exodus is one critical historical moment in our salvation history.

A second critical historical moment is the first century of our Christian era. Jesus said, "I am the bread of life." In his letters Paul meditated on the tradition handed on to him and us. The lamb the Hebrews ate on the night of their deliverance prefigured the Lamb, Jesus, who delivers us from death and nothingness, and gifts us with eternal life.

The Last Supper began Jesus's own exodus or passage from this earthly life through the darkness of death into a heavenly reality. And every Eucharist rekindles the expectation of final liberation: the Messiah will come again in glory. We pray in the Eucharist, "Until he comes again." And in the Our Father, we ask, "Thy kingdom come."

A third critical historical moment in salvation history is our Eucharistic celebration. Jesus at the Last Supper washed the feet of the disciples—an example of service. As I have done, Jesus said, so must you do. Jesus acted out a gesture we should imitate in our lives: washing the feet of one another, so to speak.

The bread we eat or the cup from which we drink isn't simply for us alone; it is meant to create a more vibrant faith community. Saint Paul wrote, "Because the loaf of bread is one, we, though many, are one body, for we all partake of the one loaf." (1 Cor. 10:17) The living Christ who nourishes me sacramentally also nourishes our fellow parishioners. And the same living Christ also nourishes countless millions around the globe.

Yes, the Eucharist challenges us to go out into our communities and to become, as best we can, what I would call "transformational agents."

Just as Jesus Christ was a transformational agent in salvation history, God calls us, his disciples, to be his fellow coworkers, agents of change for the better, in building up the kingdom of God until Jesus Christ comes again in glory at the End Times. We, as coworkers with God, have to do our best to transform prejudice into fairness, hate into peace, indifference into compassion, sorrow into joy, despair into hope, self-centeredness into other centeredness, greed into generosity, and loneliness into community. There are 101 different ways to become transformational agents, if we think about it.

One way to begin doing this in our homes, workplaces, parishes, and neighborhoods is to go out from this eucharistic celebration and keep on doing all the good we can, for all the people we can, as long as ever we can.

Nineteenth Sunday in Ordinary Time

A while back in New York City, I got an unusual request. A fellow asked whether I would celebrate a liturgy for his Maltese dog, who had just died. I replied, "I'm afraid we don't celebrate liturgies for animals." But I added, because I do like dogs, "The neighborhood nondenominational church might conduct a prayer service."

The fellow offhandedly asked, "Do you think five thousand dollars would be enough for the service?"

I immediately said, "Why didn't you tell me the dog was Catholic? I'll be happy to do it myself."

It's amazing how one line can dramatically change things.

Today's word of God carries us back in our imaginations to the ninth century before Jesus (800s) and to a prophet named Elijah. In this passage, Elijah definitely wasn't having a nice day. In fact, he told God that things were so bad that he simply wanted to die. Elijah was on the run because the king of Israel wanted to kill him. He was in the wilderness, hungry for food and drink. And lo and behold, an angel, a messenger of God, miraculously appeared and satisfied a hungry and thirsty Elijah. This development reenergized and recommitted Elijah to continue doing God's work.

The author may have challenged us to persevere in doing all the good we can, for all the people we can, and as long as ever we can, even when we don't feel like doing it. Sometimes we may even feel like Elijah, sitting underneath our own so-called proverbial tree and feeling sorry for ourselves. We may have suffered a loss, perhaps through a family divorce, death, unemployment, or family estrangement. Or we are seriously ill or disappointed with someone we counted on. Or maybe there are things we've been struggling with for years—without much success.

This story invites us, like Elijah, to get back on our feet, so to speak, and engage fully in life. Yes, all kinds of people brood about their bad luck and want to write their tombstone epitaphs. But not so fast. Listen, like Elijah, to the voice of God and let God reenergize us so we can persevere in always trying to do the right thing.

In his letter to the Christian community at Ephesus in Turkey, Paul said the Spirit of God in the waters of baptism has sealed or marked us as sons and daughters of God; yes, we belong to Jesus Christ. Hence Paul challenged the Ephesians and us to practice virtues such as forgiveness, honesty, courage, compassion, and faith or trust in God. Paul urged us to reflect in our everyday attitudes and behavior the glory or presence of God.

And in the Gospel according to John, Jesus said he was the bread of life who can transform us into new creatures. Jesus worked a sign or a wonder; he multiplied the loaves and fishes. He satisfied the hungry crowd.

As a community of disciples, we nourish our spiritual lives at the table of the Lord with the bread of life. But we also nourish our spiritual lives with the word of God.

Did you ever ask whether God speaks with us? In fact, he does. God speaks with us through the inspired word of God, the Bible, a privileged form of conversation between God and us, a two-way conversation. That's why we should be ever attentive to the word of God, especially in the liturgy. God authored the Bible in the sense that the Bible includes what God wants us to know about God, the universe, and us.

But the human authors of the Bible were real authors. They employed the language, images, literary genres, and world views they knew in their own cultures to communicate religious truths, not scientific truths.

Second, the Bible isn't one book but a library of books: prose and poetry, fiction and history, myths and legends, historical narratives and short stories, genealogies and sermons, parables and letters, songs and codes of law, blessings and curses, prophetic and proverbial sayings and apocalyptic visions. Some books in the Bible evolved over decades;

others did so over centuries. In fact, at least forty different authors wrote the Bible over fifteen hundred years. They aren't always easily understandable. That's why we have Bible study classes.

Third, I invite you to read the Bible prayerfully. We read not to find specific answers to questions the biblical authors never thought about but to become the kind of person for our day that Jesus was for his day.

Finally, one challenge today is biblical fundamentalism. Catholics and many fundamentalists do agree about certain beliefs—for example, Jesus is completely human and completely divine. We also believe in the mystery of the incarnation. But biblical fundamentalists say every word in the Bible is to be understood literally. That's not so for Catholics.

We say, for example, that the sun rises or sets. Actually the sun doesn't rise or set; these phrases are simply a way of speaking. Hence we must know what kind of literary genre the biblical authors were employing so we can discover what God was trying to say to us through a particular literary genre.

Catholics say that the two creation stories communicate certain religious truths: God is our awesome Creator, we are mere creatures, and everything God created is good. Man and woman were made in the image of God, but they broke their friendship with God and often choose their worst, evil, over their better selves. We call this fall from grace "original sin."

But how did the biblical author communicate these religious truths about creation? Through the ancient Near Eastern mythologies he knew.

The global Catholic Church is a biblical community of disciples in the sense that it acknowledges and proclaims the Bible as the word of God in human form. In particular, the scriptures point to Jesus of Nazareth as the unique or definitive revelation of God to us.

In other words, everything God ever wanted to do for us or say to us God did and said in Jesus of Nazareth. In this sense, there will be no new revelation. However, the church as a community of disciples is the instrument of the Spirit, who guides us along the journey to eternal life in the light of new problems in new generations and in new cultures. And so the inspired word of God speaks to us today.

God says to us through Elijah to persevere in doing all the good we can, for all the people we can, as long as ever we can. Through Paul,

God says to us that we belong to Christ and hence practice virtue. And through John, God invites us to nourish our spiritual lives through the Eucharist, the bread of life. But God also nourishes us through his inspired word, a privileged form of conversation between God and us.

The Bible enables us to enter into a relationship with God through Jesus Christ with the guidance of the Spirit. That's why we encourage you to check the bulletin for details about Bible classes. God is speaking to us; are we listening?

Twentieth Sunday in Ordinary Time

During the presidential campaign, I began to think, *How did politicians two hundred years ago get feedback? How did they poll?* They had no telephones, TVs, e-mails, or Facebook. Here's what I learned. Two hundred years ago politicians dispatched their assistants to local taverns, telling them to "go sip some ale" and listen. Many assistants were dispatched here and there: "Go sip here" and "Go sip there." And guess what? The words "go sip" eventually became the word "gossip." So today's polling may simply be a high-tech form of gossip. Who knows?

I have one story. A youngster said to his grandfather, "Grandpa, make a sound like a frog."

Grandpa asked, "Why do you want me to make a sound like a frog?"

The kid replied, "Because I heard Mommy and Daddy say, as soon as you croak, we're going to Disney World."

So watch what you say around youngsters. They often tell it as it is.

Today's word of God carries us back in our imaginations to the wisdom literature of ancient Israel, to the book of Proverbs. This book has about 375 wise sayings about how to live and behave. Our grandparents probably had plenty of wise sayings: "Haste makes waste." "A stitch in time saves nine." "Penny wise, pound foolish." The author personified wisdom as a woman. Wisdom oversees the mysteries of the universe, and in her hands are the secrets of life. In this passage wisdom set a table with delicious foods and fine wines. And she invited us to sit down at this table so we can nourish our souls with true wisdom; yes, this is the wisdom that distinguishes what's important from what's unimportant in life so we can realize our authentic potential, our true destiny. That's life forever in the presence of God and with God's many splendid creatures.

The wisdom author may have asked whether we have our priorities straight, first things first. Do we seek first the things of God? Do we have good relationships not only with God but also with the people who touch our lives every day? If not, how are we going to mend those relationships today?

In his letter to the Christian community at Ephesus in Turkey, Paul invited us to live a life worthy of our calling, to glorify and praise God in our everyday lives. Don't act like fools, Paul wrote. Make the most of every opportunity.

Here's a quotation that always reenergizes me, often attributed to Stephen Grellet: "I shall pass through this world but once: any good that I can do or any kindness that I can show to any human being, let me do it now, let me not defer or neglect it for I shall not pass this way again." In other words, don't live a life of regrets.

Paul urged us to make the most of every opportunity to do something good for others. And in the Gospel according to John, Jesus spoke of himself as the living bread that came down from heaven. "Whoever eats this bread and drinks from this cup," Jesus said, "abides in me and I in them." That's the mystery of the indwelling of God in us.

The Gospels have proclaimed that Jesus is the living bread come down from heaven. But the Jews quarreled among themselves about Jesus. In fact, Jesus often appeared in the Gospels, arguing with or confronting his critics about who he was or what he was teaching.

We, too, like Jesus, face conflict or confrontation of one kind or another in our daily lives. Such conflicts or arguments are not only inevitable; they can make for even better relationships. Yes, an argument can be an opportunity to clear the air, to set things back on course, or to strengthen a relationship.

Some people avoid conflict at all costs. They think nice people don't get angry; happy couples don't argue. Today we realize that arguments can be a positive experience. Let me highlight some rules for arguing fairly:

1. When we have a bone to pick with someone, set up a time to settle the matter as soon as possible. Why? We don't want to

bottle up our anger indefinitely. Setting an agreeable time and quiet place allows us to cool off and sort out the issue.

2. Define carefully the particular behavior we object to. Many arguments get sidetracked because people are unable to address the real issue. We might ask ourselves, "What do I really object to? Am I overreacting? Is it worth arguing about?" For example, when I have to clean up someone else's mess in the kitchen, it's more work for me. Always make "I" statements rather than "you" statements. "I" statements avoid name calling (like "You're inconsiderate"), generalizations ("You never think of anyone else") and abusive language ("Listen, you airhead"). It's okay to agree to disagree.

3. Express your feelings honestly. A wife whose husband was always late for dinner without texting showed her annoyance one night by leaving him a plate of dog food to eat. She obviously was expressing her feelings through the dog food plate, and fortunately her husband was good humored about it. But disguising our feelings, instead of expressing them honestly and directly, can be dangerous. An angry person, for example, can give the silent treatment. Feelings are neither positive nor negative; they are facts. Just as aches and pains in our bodies alert us to physical problems, feelings alert us to problems in our relationships. There's nothing wrong with expressing our feelings honestly and calmly. I know some of you may be thinking, *If only it were that easy.*

4. Come up with creative solutions. The goal of any conflict or argument is to resolve a problem in a way that is agreeable to both parties. You may have a specific request that will resolve the issue; for example, "How about playing your drums or trombone some time other than midnight?" Many times, though, we cannot think of a mutually acceptable solution. Then we brainstorm for solutions. The more ideas, the better. The important thing is that both sides work together to solve the problem.

There are other so-called rules for fighting fairly. These include actively listening to what the other person is saying, staying calm, agreeing to disagree, and so forth. Saint Paul wrote, "Love does not brood over injuries." All of us must be willing to forgive, forget, apologize, and move on with our lives. This, of course, is a two-way street.

If we have fun together, do things together, and communicate regularly, we create a climate of love, respect, and trust that will foster positive relationships.

When all else fails, turn to chapter 6 in the Gospel according to Luke: "Be merciful, just as your Father is merciful. Stop judging and you will not be judged. Stop condemning and you will not be condemned. Forgive and you will be forgiven." (Luke 6:36-37)

Twenty-First Sunday in Ordinary Time

You may have heard the story of the woman who went to see her rabbi and said, "Rabbi, I have something terrible to tell you. My husband is poisoning me."

The surprised rabbi asked, "How do you know that?"

The woman replied, "I'm telling you, he's poisoning me. What should I do?"

The rabbi then suggested, "Let me talk to your husband."

A week later the rabbi called the woman and said, "Well, I spoke to your husband on the phone for six hours. You want my advice?"

The woman said, "Of course."

The rabbi replied, "Take the poison."

I suppose the moral of the story is, not all advice is good.

The word of God takes us back over three thousand years to the Middle East and to a charismatic leader named Joshua. The book of Joshua begins the religious history of ancient Israel. The Hebrews were in the Promised Land, and some of the indigenous people had become Hebrew. And so Joshua called the people together and challenged them to make a choice: serve—in other words, worship—the God who had worked signs and wonders in their lives or serve false gods. Joshua renewed his covenantal commitment to God alone. And so did the Hebrews. The author invited us to do the same: to renew our baptismal promises to God alone; yes, to live a life worthy of our calling as sons and daughters of God, our Father.

And in the Gospel according to John, Jesus challenged the disciples to make a choice: believe in him as God's holy One, the One who descended from heaven and will ascend to heaven. This is the bread of life, the presence of the living Christ sacramentally in the signs of bread and wine, who by the power of the Spirit nourishes us spiritually in our earthly journey toward our heavenly home. And what was the decision these disciples made? Some simply walked away; others stayed. "Master," they asked, "to whom shall we go? You have the words of eternal life."

As disciples of Jesus, do we believe Jesus is indeed God's holy One, our way, our truth and our life? In his letter to the Christian community at Ephesus, Paul wrote about the relationship between husband and wife. And while alluding to the Greco-Roman household codes of his day, Paul transcended these codes and compared marriage to the relationship of Jesus Christ to the church: a self-giving love.

In light of Paul's letter to the Ephesians, I would like to reflect briefly on the sacrament of marriage. Now there are all kinds of literature about marriage. Let me begin with a story about two old friends who were catching up on one another's comings and goings over drinks at a sidewalk café.

"To be perfectly honest," one began, "I have spent years looking for the perfect woman. In fact, I met a very lovely and highly intelligent woman. But I discovered that she was terribly self-centered. Then I met a woman who was outgoing and generous. But she was a spendthrift. I had just about given up on ever meeting the perfect woman until one day I met her: beautiful, intelligent, kind, generous, and a wonderful sense of humor. She was the perfect woman."

"So why didn't you marry her?" his friend asked.

Looking down at his glass, he replied, "Because she was looking for the perfect man."

Often people look for the perfect "this" or "that" and forget that life isn't perfect. Often we have to muddle through messes and make the best of things. Marriage is a risk. Like most things in life, we have to continually work at a relationship.

If we think a relationship is getting stale, randomly surprise the other person with something he or she enjoys—for example, theater or sports tickets or dinner at a favorite restaurant. Marriage calls for time together to enjoy one another's company. It calls for a commitment despite the highs and lows of everyday life. It requires good communication, active listening, empathetic feelings, and positive behavior. And it's okay to agree to disagree sometimes. Like any relationship, it inevitably involves conflict.

We have to forgive mistakes and move on together. Above all, marriage takes three to last: two best friends and a God who loves us for who we are. I've heard some metaphors for marriage—for example, partner and soul mate. But my favorite is "best friend" to laugh with, live for, and love. The only way to have friends is to be one. I would like to highlight three ingredients I think will help people live together as best friends for life:

First is sense of humor. The nineteenth-century English novelist William Thackeray (we had to read his novel *Vanity Fair*) wrote that humor is "a mixture of love and wit." We all need a sense of humor—not always, of course, for we can't take lightly the illness or death of loved ones. We do at times have to take ourselves seriously but not always. We have to be able to smile at those little and large eccentricities in ourselves and in loved ones (and we all have eccentricities if we look closely)—from the way someone slurps soup to the time taken to get ready to go somewhere—for life is full of contradictions. Yes, we can be exciting and boring, trusting and suspicious, selfless and selfish. We have to expect inconsistencies in ourselves, other people, and the world about us. And we have to laugh about these inconsistencies.

Yes, humor is indeed a mixture of love and wit. And always keep these truisms in mind:

- Life isn't fair, but it's still good.
- It's okay to get angry with God because he can take it.
- Don't let the sun go down on your anger; sort out the issue honestly, calmly, and quickly.
- It's never too late to be happy, but it's up to you.
- Get outside every day because miracles are waiting everywhere.

Second, we need a sense of wonder. We need to be continually surprised, delighted, and amazed at life. Amazed at what? Amazed, first of all, that we are alive. Alive to the universe around us—flowers and trees, landscapes and waterscapes, sunrises and sunsets, friends and children. Alive to the fact that God lives within each one of us in a community of disciples. And yes, amazed at that first encounter with one another that blossomed into a marriage as best friends.

Third, we need to develop a sense of the other. Marriage can last through good times and bad, through sickness and health, because best friends have a ceaseless sense of the other. Never put job or profession before family. Concern for each other impels us to reach out to people around us.

Mother Teresa of Calcutta captured for me the power of love in this passage from a speech she gave in 1988 to Gonzaga College High School graduates in Washington, D.C.:

> I saw a man sitting and looking most terrible and so I went to him and shook his hand. He looked up and said, "Oh, what a long, long time since I felt the warmth of a human hand." He brightened up, he was so full of joy that there was somebody that loved him, somebody who cared.

There's the power of touch! And so let us reflect. I pray that all our relationships and friendships might be imbued with a sense of humor, a sense of wonder, and a sense of the other.

Twenty-Second Sunday in Ordinary Time

You may have heard the story of the minister, priest, and rabbi who were kibitzing about death and dying in the clubhouse after a day of golfing. And one of them asked, "When you're in your casket, and friends and parishioners are mourning you, what would you like them to say?"

The minister said, "I would like them to say I was a good family man, a deeply spiritual human being, and a caring pastor."

The priest replied, "I would like them to say I was a good preacher, a prayerful celebrant of the mysteries of God, and a compassionate counselor to my parishioners."

The rabbi paused for a while and then said, "I'd like them to say, 'Look, he's moving!'"

Now there are three different perspectives on death.

The word of God carries us back in our imaginations well over three thousand years to an address of Moses in the book of Deuteronomy. The word *Deuteronomy* is a Greek word that means the "second law." Moses pled with the Hebrews, about to enter the Promised Land, to be faithful to the demands of their covenantal promises. Yes, God entered into a special relationship with the Hebrews and promised blessings but only if they kept God's laws. In other words, they worshipped God and treated their fellow human beings fairly. That word may be asking whether we recognize our absolute dependency on God by worshipping God and treating our fellow human beings fairly.

The author of the letter of James was a very practical man. He boldly said there shouldn't be a discrepancy between faith and action.

He wanted action, not words. He asked us: are we only hearers of the Word of God? Or are we doers as well? This is true religion. God's word challenges us to be doers as well as hearers of God's word. And we have a particular responsibility to care for the vulnerable and needy, whoever they are. But do we?

In the Gospel according to Mark, Jesus distinguished between the external behavior of the scribes and Pharisees, and their internal attitudes. They were hypocrites, Jesus said. The word *hypocrite* etymologically means "an actor": this is one who says one thing and actually does another. Hypocrites publicly condemn behavior they do privately. The media highlights this hypocrisy often. Hypocrites are careful to observe the right etiquette (they pay lip service to God), but internally (in their hearts) they're thinking immoral thoughts—for example, greed, dishonesty, lust, envy, and pride. Jesus asked us whether we are like the scribes and Pharisees, saying one thing in public and doing the opposite in private.

This Gospel seems to say human beings are a bundle of contradictions. Yes, who really are we? Why were we born? It was no accident. And if it wasn't, our lives must have meaning. Leo Tolstoy, the nineteenth-century Russian novelist and author of such classic literature as *War and Peace* and *The Death of Ivan Ilyich*, wrote a book called *A Confession*, in which he described his own search for meaning and purpose. Yes, "where did I come from?" "Where am I going?" "Who am I?" and "What is my life all about?" Tolstoy discovered that many ordinary people were able to answer these questions much better than he could through their faith. They had a relationship with God through Jesus Christ by the power of the Spirit. That friendship with God gave their lives meaning and purpose. Jesus was indeed their way, truth, and life.

A while ago, I was leafing through Daniel Levinson's *The Seasons of a Man's Life*, a one-time national best seller. The book is about the cycle of human development: young adulthood, middle years, and late adulthood.

As we go through this cycle, we continually face crises of one kind or another. The word *crisis* has a twofold meaning; it can be a moment of disaster or a moment of opportunity. I prefer the latter meaning: a moment of opportunity. And as we go through this cycle, we are constantly letting go of the past so we can move forward. But move forward to where?

We, of course, believe we're moving forward into a more intense life with God—our true destiny. Time and again, we have to let go—we have to let go of friends, loved ones, perhaps health or job. And ultimately we will have to let go of our earthly lives in a leap of faith into the hands of an all-loving God. That final letting go is like a trapeze performer at a circus.

Just as these acrobats trust in the skills of their fellow acrobats when they let go of their rope in midair, so too do we trust in God's mercy that he will catch us as we let go of our lives in that final leap into the darkness of death. Our earthly life, from a Catholic point of view, is simply a journey, a pilgrimage toward an intense life with God forever.

So where are we going? What are we living for? There are as many answers to these questions as there are people. We cannot adequately answer these questions, and yet we cannot help but answer them by the way in which we live and what we do.

On the one hand we are finite and mortal; we came out of nothingness at one particular time, and we will fall back into nothingness at another particular time. On the other hand, we are free within limits and accountable for the way we live.

Whether we are powerful or powerless, rich or poor, no matter how great our intellect, no matter how noble our birth pedigree, the purpose of life is to be in a relationship with God. That's why we are here: to be in a relationship, a friendship, with God forever.

The Catholic answer to the question "Why are we here?" acknowledges the brevity of human life. It also acknowledges our freedom to choose good over evil, right over wrong, the true over the false. And hence all of us are responsible, accountable, for the way in which we choose to live. Tragically, people, in fact, do choose evil over good, wrong over right.

Why? Because there's something not quite right with us. Things are out of kilter, broken. The story of the beginnings of man and woman in the book of Genesis highlights this brokenness. The Catholic tradition calls this "original sin."

In fact, things seem to be quite messy in many regions of our globe. Rebels create havoc, jihadists terrorize innocent people, and millions of refugees flee violence in search of a better and more stable life. Yes, human beings cry out for freedom, peace, justice, and truth. They cry out for healing, redemption, and salvation.

But who can heal us, save us? Some, of course, have sought human solutions to these human problems. They have looked for answers in the world of things, in other persons, and in "isms" of one kind or another.

The Catholic tradition looks beyond the world of things to a power beyond ourselves.

This awesome and overwhelming power beyond ourselves—God—isn't indifferent to our human situation, for our God is a compassionate God. This compassionate power beyond ourselves—God—became flesh in Jesus of Nazareth and is alive by the power of the Spirit in our midst today. It is especially alive in the community of disciples we call the church and in the sacramental signs of water, bread, wine, and oil. God's love for us is as crazy as the love of the father for the son in the parable of the prodigal son.

Yes, we possess within our fragile selves the incredible treasure of God's life. We are in a relationship with God by virtue of the life-giving waters of baptism. But we must continue to struggle, as the prophet Micah said centuries ago, to do the right, love goodness, and walk humbly with our God. There's still that "pull" within us to do the opposite.

Salvation, like the words *healing* and *restoring to right order*, describes an overwhelming good, a good beyond our wildest imaginations who breathes God's life into us so we can see God as God really is, face-to-face.

The letter of James today speaks about the Word that can save our souls. That Word, who was with God, became flesh in Jesus of Nazareth, and was transformed into a new heavenly reality, will also lift us up into that new heavenly reality where we will be in a relationship with God forever.

Twenty-Third Sunday in Ordinary Time

Labor Day, a national holiday since 1894, was founded to promote the dignity of human work.

Joseph, the carpenter, is our model. Isn't it interesting that God put the protection of Jesus and Mary in the hands of a common laborer, who worked with his hands and wood?

Our modern popes, from Leo XIII to John XXIII and John Paul II, have emphasized that economic models exist for the person and not the person for these models. They reasoned that all people have the right to productive work and decent working conditions. In fact, John Paul II condemned those economic models that generate profits at the expense of the dignity of the person. Yes, Labor Day invites us to take pride in our work.

There's an ancient wisdom tradition that says God sends each person into this life with a special message to deliver, a special song to sing for others, a special act of love to bestow. No matter who we are, no matter what we do, whether extraordinary or ordinary, all of us, from a Christian perspective, have a mission to fulfill. God has committed some work to each of us that he has not committed to another. And so whatever our life's work is, do it well. And isn't that what holiness is all about—doing whatever is our life's work as best we can?

You may have heard about President William Henry Harrison's inaugural address in 1841. It was the longest inaugural address ever, over two hours. Harrison, sixty-seven years of age, gave the address on a cold, wintry day without hat or coat. And guess what? He caught a cold that turned into pneumonia. And one month later he was dead. The lesson is simple enough: if you're too long winded, you may kill yourself. Let that be a lesson for all speakers.

Now if you're a horse-racing fan, or even if you're not, you've probably heard of Seabiscuit, Horse of the Year in 1938. The story of Seabiscuit eventually became a national best seller and film.

Seabiscuit wasn't a beautiful horse—he was small, had crooked legs, and was labeled a loser because he began his career with sixteen losses. But a trainer saw a quality in this horse that convinced him Seabiscuit could be a winner; he also persuaded a millionaire to buy the horse for $7,500. The two hired a washed-up prizefighter, Red Pollard, as the jockey. A naturally gifted horseman, Pollard, too, sensed in Seabiscuit the heart of a champion and quickly bonded with the horse.

Somehow, these three people saw greatness in each other and in the horse that had eluded everyone else, and they worked with Seabiscuit. Despite absurd odds, Seabiscuit began to win and win, and he captivated a country in the midst of the 1930s Depression.

The story of Seabiscuit is really a story of ephphatha (the Aramaic word in today's gospel), an openness to greatness. That spirit is contagious. God recognizes the possibilities for spiritual greatness within us and other people. He has made us "living temples of the holy Spirit." (1 Cor. 6:19) In the waters of baptism, God breathes his Spirit into us, and the power of the Spirit enables us to continue the work of Jesus: to be instruments of God's compassion, generosity, love, and forgiveness to the people around us, including our families, colleagues in the workplace, relatives, and neighbors. And the result of that spiritual greatness is character, our moral character, the kind of person we are.

Now the word of God from Isaiah—a message of hope for an eighth century of anxious people—describes a new age in which we will experience God in our midst, a God who heals, refreshes, and calms our anxieties. Anxiety is like a rocking chair. It gives us something to do but gets us nowhere.

Isaiah spoke about a new age in which the blind will see, the deaf will hear, and the rivers will overflow. Yes, the Messiah will come. God's word asks us to remember that in times of darkness, God is our light. In times of brokenness, God is our healer; and in times of discouragement, God is our hope.

The letter of James urges us to practice two fundamental principles of justice. "Show no partiality"; we must treat every human being with the same respect, from the beginning of life to the end of life. And the second principle is called "God's preferential option for the poor." Jesus said we will be judged by our response to the hungry, the thirsty, the stranger, the naked, and the prisoner. In other words what we do to others we do to Jesus.

In the Gospel according to Mark. Jesus encountered a deaf man, made time for him, and took him to a quiet, safe place. Jesus then "puts his finger into the man's ears and, spitting, touched his tongue." Notice, he used no exam gloves. But Jesus didn't just cure the man with a fleeting word. By his touch, Jesus entered into this person's struggle and, in doing so, brought hope and healing into this man's life.

The Aramaic word *ephphatha* can mean "be open" or "be released." Jesus "released" the man not only from his disability but also from his isolation. May our prayer may be that we are released from our fears, released from a self-centeredness that makes us "deaf" to hearing God, and "mute" in responding to someone in need. And may our prayer also be that we be open to the possibilities for spiritual greatness within us and others. Every day opportunities to do good open up to us, but do we seize these daily opportunities to do good?

The letter of James, in particular, speaks about our moral character. Character defines who we are at the core of our inmost self; that's where, to paraphrase St. Augustine, we are what we are.

People of moral character will choose fair-mindedness over bigotry, the person over impersonal business or material advantage, genuine respect and forgiveness over the lust for pleasure or power. They will speak up for what is right and defend what is fair; they will stand for something.

They will choose excellence and quality, when faced with a choice between excellence and quality or what is slipshod or just enough to do a job. Yes, they will do their best to make something "just right" because it is the better and worthier thing to do.

The word of God urges us to have a heart, to always seek what is right and good. And having found what is right and good, as the Nike advertisement says, we should "just do it," for within each of us is the heart of a spiritual champion.

Twenty-Fourth Sunday in Ordinary Time

I read in a "Dear Abby" column about a couple ready to leave for a twenty-fifth college reunion. The husband looked into the mirror on the way out. He wasn't happy with what he saw and said, "Honey, I weigh too much, and I have a double chin, a potbelly, a bald head, a wrinkled face, and clothes that don't fit. I don't feel good about myself. I need you to pay me a compliment."

And the wife replied, "Your eyesight is perfect."

Now, that's a backhanded compliment.

The word of God takes us back in our imaginations to the sixth century before Jesus, to Deutero-Isaiah or the second section of the book of Isaiah. The author spoke about a mysterious servant of God in this song. Now the sixth century was a catastrophe for the Hebrews; they'd lost their kingdom, king, and temple in Jerusalem. Some were murdered, and others were deported to Babylonia (modern Iraq).

In this song, this mysterious servant of God, despite all kinds of physical and verbal abuse, persevered in carrying out the mission God had entrusted to him. The early Christian community saw in this servant Jesus the suffering Messiah. The book of Isaiah challenges us to persevere in our lives of discipleship with Jesus as the servant in Isaiah did.

Perseverance often makes the difference between success or failure. The basketball legend Michael Jordan is a good example. All he ever wanted to do was play basketball, but when he was a high school sophomore, the coach cut him from the team. Suddenly he couldn't play. When the team went to the district tournament, Jordan asked whether he could ride along on the bus. The coach agreed if Jordan would carry the team uniforms. Michael Jordan said later to the *Chicago Tribune*, "It's probably good that it happened. It made me know what disappointment felt like. And I knew that I didn't want to have that feeling ever again."

Michael Jordan didn't give up. That summer he practiced every day. Next year he made the varsity team and then went to the University of North Carolina, and the rest is history. Yes, the book of Isaiah challenges us to persevere in our lives of discipleship with Jesus.

The letter of James says simply that we should practice what we believe. Our faith in Jesus should compel us to reach out compassionately to other people and to give our time, talents, and yes, perhaps even some of our treasure to people, especially the needy.

And in the Gospel according to Mark, Jesus asked, "Who do you say that I am?" (Mark 8:29) It sounds kind of like one of those polls during campaign season. "Yes," Jesus asked us, "who do you say I am?" In other words, what does Jesus mean to me? What do I mean to Jesus?

The Gospel writers give us four different portraits or faces of Jesus because they wrote to four different audiences and emphasized four different ways in which to follow Jesus. Jesus was a rabbi or teacher in Matthew; so, too, should we be teachers, especially by example, by the practice of virtue.

Jesus was a suffering Messiah in Mark; so, too, may we cope with illness or disability, or make sacrifices. And yes, we may even wonder at times whether God has forgotten us, especially if what's happening is the opposite of what we want to happen.

Jesus was a healer or peacemaker in Luke; so should we be as well in our relationships with one another. To be a disciple, for Luke especially, is not only to be a hearer of God's Word. But like Mary, the disciple par excellence, it means being a doer of God's word.

Jesus was our friend in John; so, too, should we become his friend, especially in prayer.

What is your favorite image of Jesus? Do you even have one? What image inspires you to become the kind of person Jesus was in his day? Perhaps the larger question may be, how did the early Christian community see Jesus? They initially saw Jesus as the fulfillment of the hopes of ancient Israel. And so they named him the Messiah, the Christos, the anointed one.

But the more they reflected on who he was, the more they saw Jesus not only as the fulfillment of their hopes but also as the foundation of their hopes, the eternal Word. The Gospel according to John captures this image magnificently in the prologue: "In the beginning was the Word and the Word," and so forth. Yes, Jesus was the foundation as well as the fulfillment of their hopes as well as our own.

Who, then, was Jesus, with whom we seek a relationship? He was a real historical person, flesh and blood like us. He experienced, as we sometimes do, fatigue, hunger, satisfaction, joy, friendship, anger, disappointment, and loneliness.

He was a rabbi, a teacher, and a prophet who preached that the kingdom of God was breaking into our lives. He worked signs and wonders, proclaiming that good ultimately would triumph over evil. He possessed authority to forgive wrongdoings; he promised eternal life.

He had a unique relationship with the God of ancient Israel. In fact, he was one with God, true God and true man; but he was crucified, he died, and then he was raised up from the dead. He is alive and in our midst today, especially in the sacramental life of the church, the community of disciples.

Jesus taught not only that the kingdom of God was breaking into our lives but also that we can share in this kingdom of God by living out lives of discipleship with Jesus. How? By living prayerfully in the presence of God; by recognizing that our lives have an ultimate purpose; by seeing in Jesus—the Word made flesh—the face of God; by reaching out compassionately to the people who touch our lives every day; by experiencing the presence of the living Christ in our sacramental life; and by always being ready to let go of our earthly lives, in the mystery of death, so we can be one with God in glory forever. Lastly, Jesus taught that God is our Father, a compassionate God who is always near us at the start of each day to guide us on our pathway to our heavenly home.

I close with an old Chinese story about a mother whose only son died suddenly. In her grief, she pleaded with a Buddhist monk renowned for his holy life. "With what prayers, what magical incantations, can you bring my son back to life?"

The monk told her, "Find me a mustard seed from a home that has never known sorrow. We will use the mustard seed to drive the grief out of your life."

And so the woman set off in search of such a magical mustard seed. But wherever she stopped, in homes or mansions, she found one tale after another of woe and misfortune. And she became so involved in helping other people overcome their grief that she actually forgot her own quest for that magical mustard seed, realizing gradually that it had in fact driven the grief out of her own life.

As disciples of Jesus, we, too, will experience pain, grief, and disappointment in our own lives. But Jesus challenges to take up our daily crosses and to become the kind of person today that Jesus was in his day. For the only Gospel some people may ever read is us, how we live our everyday lives.

Twenty-Fifth Sunday in Ordinary Time

Pope Francis is a friendly, compassionate face for the church universal. He is definitely not a fire-and-brimstone preacher. You may have heard about a fire-and-brimstone preacher who thundered from the pulpit, "Everyone in this parish is going to die." An elderly man burst out laughing. Annoyed, the preacher repeated even louder, "I said, everyone in this parish is going to die." And again, the man laughed. The preacher shouted, "What's so funny about that?"

And the man answered, "I don't belong to this parish." So much for misreading tea leaves.

The word of God takes us back to the wisdom literature of ancient Israel. The author spoke about a person who always tried to do what was right and fair. But how did some so-called evildoers react? They wanted to murder him. Let's see whether God will rescue him, they said.

The word raises the eternal problem of evil. Why do the wicked sometimes seem to prosper and the good suffer? Or, to put it another way, why do bad things happen to good people? There's no satisfactory answer. But the word assures us that God is close to us, even when God seems far away.

The author of the letter of James asked, "Why do some people choose evil? Why greed at the expense of others, why random violence, blatant thievery." People do indeed at times choose wrong over right, falsehood over truth. Why? Catholic Christianity says people are basically good, but that there is something not quite right with us. There are tensions at the core of our being: between self and others as well as between rational and irrational, responsible and irresponsible behavior.

Christianity calls this human condition "original sin." Quite simply, that is a lack of a relationship with God, a fall from grace described in Genesis. "They hid from God." This is why human beings cry out for a relationship with God. Saint Augustine, one of the great intellectual stars in early Christianity, sums this up poetically: "You have made us for yourself, O Lord, and our heart is restless until it rests in God." And Jesus, the Word made flesh, through his life-giving ministry and terrible death and glorious resurrection reestablished a relationship with God.

We are by grace what Jesus is by nature: sons and daughters of God, our Father. But we are also mortal. Our lives are fragile and transitory— the Bible repeatedly emphasizes this theme of mortality. I sometimes think of the fellow reading a tombstone. The inscription was "Where you stand, I once stood. And where I lie, you one day will lie."

In the Gospel according to Mark, Jesus spoke about his own mortality. Yes, he challenged us to be servant leaders. We live to serve others, and service may cost us dearly.

But then Jesus predicted his own passion, death, and resurrection. This Easter mystery reveals our true destiny: to be in a relationship with God forever in a new, indescribable, transformative life. Jesus in the Gospels brings us face-to-face with our own dying.

Death is a fact of life. Andy Rooney once wrote, "It's paradoxical how the idea of living a long life appeals to everyone, but the idea of growing old doesn't appeal to anyone."

And the experience of death today is different from, for example, one hundred years ago. Then people may have died in their forties or fifties in their homes, often with family and friends surrounding them. Today some people may die in their nineties or one hundreds in hospitals, nursing homes, or hospices.

There's a best seller *Being Mortal: Medicine and What Matters in the End* that questions whether employing medical technology to lengthen a life at the expense of quality of life is the right thing to do. Surgeon Atul Gawande describes three patterns of decline. The first results from an incurable disease; treatments may lengthen that life, but eventually the body wastes away, and death comes quickly. In the second pattern, a chronic disease, such as emphysema, is treatable, but repeated relapses eventually siphon the life out of that person. And finally there's the pattern of old age, called "frailty": no life-threatening disease but the gradual "decline" of bodily systems.

The question for this doctor becomes when to let go, when to stop offering treatments that most likely don't work. He asks, why submit the dying to the full panoply of medical procedures only to see them merely exist in institutions and completely lose their independence?

Many of us are familiar with Elisabeth Kübler-Ross's five stages, through which many dying patients and loved ones normally pass: Simply put, they are the following:

- Denial: "No, not me." This is a typical reaction if a patient learns he or she is terminally ill.
- Anger: "Why me?" God may be a special target for anger. That's okay; God can take it.
- Bargaining: "Yes me, but." The patient accepts death but bargains generally for more time.
- Depression: "Yes, me." The person mourns things not done, regret things done.
- And finally, there's acceptance: "My time is running out, but it's all right."

These stages aren't absolute but are a useful guide in understanding the behavior of those facing death. These stages also can apply to any big change in life—for example, job loss, divorce, or the death of a loved one.

Dr. Kübler-Ross wrote another book *Death: The Final Stage of Growth*. The title leads me to the Christian understanding of death. The foundation of that understanding is Good Friday/Easter. Hidden in the death of Jesus on Good Friday was the glory of his resurrection on Easter. Our faith challenges us to remember that the light of our resurrection will shatter the darkness of our own deaths.

The story of Jesus didn't end in the tragedy of the cross but in the triumph of the resurrection, when the God-man, Jesus, transfigured or transformed into an indescribable heavenly reality. The risen Christ anticipates what we one day will become.

Let's be honest. Most of us don't long with Saint Paul to be free from this earthly life so that we can be with the Risen Christ. Nor are we like Saint Francis of Assisi, who welcomed Sister Death in his "Canticle of the Creatures": "Praise to you, my Lord, for our sister bodily death."

Many pass through the stages Elisabeth Kübler-Ross describes. There is a darkness about death that even Jesus cried out against. Yet in the Christian vision of things, we expect that the Spirit of God, who continually amazes us, will surprise us in the moment of our own dying with a new, indescribable heavenly reality.

I close with a line from Erma Bombeck, who wrote with humor, "When I stand before God at the end of my life, I would hope that I would not have a single bit of talent left, and could say, 'I used everything you gave me.'" That indeed is a good preparation for the reality of death.

Twenty-Sixth Sunday in Ordinary Time

How many of you heard that Pope Francis addressed the joint session of our United States Congress? He highlighted four representatives of the American people. A nation can be considered great, he underscored, when it stands for "freedom" as Lincoln did; when it enables people to "dream of full rights" as Martin Luther King sought to do; when it strives for "justice and the cause of the oppressed" as Dorothy Day did; and when it has "openness to God" in prayer and dialogue between peoples and religions as Thomas Merton was. And then the Pope said, "Let us remember the Golden Rule: 'Do unto others as you would have them do unto you.'"

And what about the inspiring Mass, which many other clergy and I concelebrated with Pope Francis at my alma mater, The Catholic University? The pope quoted Junipero Serra, a fellow Franciscan friar: *"siempre adelante"* or "always forward" in evangelizing people.

On another topic, I just read a story about a youngster who asked his mother,

"Where do people come from?"

His mom replied, "God made Adam and Eve, they had children, and that's where we came from."

Two days later, the youngster asked his dad, who answered, "The human race evolved from apes over millions of years."

The confused youngster went back to his mother and said, "Mommy, you told me that God created people, but Daddy says they came from apes."

His mom replied, "Well, Joey, it's very simple. I told you about my side of the family, and Daddy told you about his side of the family."

That's a good answer.

The word of God takes us back to the wanderings of the Hebrews in the wilderness after their escape, liberation, or freedom from Ancient Egypt. The book of Numbers takes its title from the numbering or census of the Hebrews. A better title for this book might have been "Grumblings." It is a long, sad story about discontentment.

Here Moses asked God to breathe his Spirit on the seventy people gathered. But God surprisingly breathed his Spirit not only on these seventy but also on two others who weren't even there. So Joshua complained to Moses, "Stop these two from prophesying, from speaking in God's name."

And Moses simply answered, "The spirit or presence of God breathes and works wherever God wants."

God's word challenges us to recognize the presence of God in the most unlikely places, most questionable people, and most improbable religious traditions. The word also invites us to pray anew for the seven gifts or energies of the Spirit already in us. These are wisdom to focus on what truly matters, our relationship with God and one another; understanding and knowledge to enter deeply into the mysteries of God and the truths of our faith; counsel to make good moral decisions; fortitude or strength of character to stand up for what is right; piety to give God, our Creator, our creaturely praise and worship; and finally, fear of the Lord or the healthy concern never to lose our friendship with God.

The author of the letter of James spoke about people who become so absorbed in earthly things that they forget their ultimate purpose: to be in a relationship with God in our earthly lives and beyond in a heavenly life. James challenged us to spend our energies—not on transitory treasures like money and power but on lasting treasures like our relationships with God and one another.

A medieval play called *Everyman* captures this theme powerfully. God asks death to tell "everyman" (who symbolizes you and me) that everyman's life on earth is over. Everyman then asks the wealth, fame, and power of his "friends" to accompany him, but they refuse. In the end, everyman gets only one friend to join him: good works. The point is simple: when death comes for us, only the good we have done will accompany us into the mystery of death.

In the Gospel according to Mark, Jesus spoke about tough love. There is one issue we should settle quickly: Jesus wasn't recommending self-mutilation. His speech was a Semitic way of speaking graphically, vividly, and exaggeratedly to make a point.

Today we might imagine Jesus saying to someone, "If your wealth should keep you from pursuing the things of God, sell your stocks and bonds and give the proceeds to the poor. Better to enter heaven without much than be condemned to Gehenna, leaving behind a substantial estate for others to argue over." Gehenna, you may know, was a smoldering garbage dump outside Jerusalem, which came to symbolize eternal punishment.

Or we might imagine Jesus saying to someone else, "If job security leads you to compromise your ethics and integrity, quit. Better to be employed elsewhere than to be thrown into Gehenna with all your benefits."

In harsh words about "cutting off" and "plucking out," not to be understood literally, Jesus dramatically called us to realize that discipleship means not letting anything—anything!—derail us in our quest for the things of God; this means not allowing the pursuit of wealth, security, or status to detach us from or diminish the love of God or the love we have for our families and loved ones.

Yes, we have to have the courage of faith to let go and remove from our lives whatever cuts us off from God, family, and loved ones. Throughout history, people have written to us and taught us about "seizing the day." Someone wrote: "Twenty years from now we will be more disappointed by the things we didn't do than by the ones we did." Think about it.

The popular lecturer Leo Buscaglia, who wrote books like *Living, Loving and Learning,* had a student who wrote a reflection during the Vietnam War with a straightforward message. "Don't regret something because you didn't do it; you only live once as the saying goes; it's the real thing; and to the extent that our lives are in our own hands, do good now, not later; don't regret not doing it as the rich man regretted not helping Lazarus." The student's reflection, titled "Things You Didn't

Do," concludes, in an ode to his father, "You put up with me and you loved me. There were lots of things I wanted to thank you for when you returned from Vietnam. But you never did return!"

That's a compelling message: don't live a life of regrets. Do good now. Quietly sit down somewhere and begin to think of your own obituary. What do you want to be remembered for?

This reminds me of a newspaper story about the Pulitzer Prize winner Rudyard Kipling, the early twentieth-century British author and poet. He subscribed to a newspaper that published an announcement of his death by mistake.

So Kipling wrote to the editor, "I've just read that I'm dead. Don't forget to delete me from your list of subscribers."

Yes, today we might ask the Spirit of God to reenergize us so we will have our priorities straight, that we won't let anything derail us from our purpose in life: to be in a relationship with God forever; and that we will try, as best we can, to live lives of no regrets.

Twenty-Seventh Sunday in Ordinary Time

On October 4, we celebrate the feast of Saint Francis of Assisi, a role model for us. Francis saw the glory-presence footprints of God everywhere, in all of God's creatures and creations.

But first here's a story. I had to be in New York recently, and while there, someone showed me a photo of myself thirty-plus years ago. My first reaction was, "Wow, what happened? I looked pretty good then." And then I began thinking. *The only time we want to get old is when we're young.*

Kids say, "I'm four and a half going on five." But I've never heard someone say, "I'm fifty-four and a half going on fifty-five."

When you're a teen, you're always jumping ahead. For example, you're "going to be" sixteen. And then you reach the great day; you're twenty-one. But then you turn thirty. It sounds funny, doesn't it? You turn. Like something turning sour.

Then you're pushing forty, putting on the brakes. You finally reach fifty. That's it. But wait, you make it to sixty. You didn't think you would. And you've built up so much momentum that you hit seventy. And in your eighties, you do this cycle each day: hit lunch, reach bedtime.

Then in the nineties, you start going backward. For example, "I was just ninety-two." And if I make it to one hundred, I guess I become a kid again: one hundred and a half going on one hundred and one.

But honestly, I try to see each day as a blessing as it unfolds. As Blessed John Henry Newman wrote in his reflection *Lead Kindly Light*, "I do not ask to see the distant scene: one step enough for me."

The word of God takes us back to the beginnings of the human family. The book of Genesis describes how God created man and woman as partners or helpmates in the service of further life, children. And although that first human family became our first dysfunctional family in the narrative about "the fall from grace," the biblical author highlighted the common bond the global human family has.

The author of the letter to the Hebrews described our spiritual family. God became human in Jesus. Jesus was indeed the face of God among us. And through his death and resurrection, God gifts us with his divine life; and so we are brothers and sisters to one another, and sons and daughters of God, our Father. God has consecrated or set us apart to be in a relationship with him forever. And our faith in Jesus Christ proclaims that one day God will transfigure us into a new heavenly life as God has already transfigured Jesus.

In the Gospel according to Mark, Jesus spoke, among other things, about the sacred relationship we call marriage. Yes, the word of God connects our human with our divine family. Family life is about spending time together in a relationship; it's about generosity, forgiveness, and love. It's about becoming other centered rather than self-centered.

But today, on the feast of Saint Francis of Assisi, since I'm a Franciscan friar and because the pope's namesake is Francis, I feel compelled to speak briefly about this thirteen-century founder of the worldwide Franciscan family.

Francis of Assisi has been portrayed as a lover of animals, an environmentalist, a flower child (see the Zeffirelli movie *Brother Sun, Sister Moon*), a peacemaker, a mystic, a reformer, and a poet. But who really was Francis?

Francis came from a middle-class Italian family. He was a dreamer and soldier; twice he went off to the wars in that region, and twice he failed miserably to find glory in them.

Then one night he had a dream that compelled him to go back to Assisi. And there he began to wrestle with the fundamental questions: What am I living for? What is the ultimate purpose of my life?

Francis yearned for something greater than himself that would give meaning to his life. Gradually, in silence and in prayer, Francis searched for God. Eventually Francis gave up "his things," so to speak.

He experienced his "creature-hood," his absolute dependency on God; and in that experience, he found everything: an all-good God who became flesh in Jesus and is alive in our midst by the power of the Spirit.

So Francis began to pursue the gospel way of life in a literal way. Eventually, men and women gathered around him, as religious and laymen and women, to live what became known as the Franciscan way of life with God.

Eight hundred years later, does Francis have anything to say to us? Of course he does. In addition to writings like his "Canticle of Brother Sun" and his "Testament," we can see his message in three particular incidents from his life.

The first took place at La Verna, near Florence, Italy, in 1224. Francis was praying, and suddenly he experienced the marks of the crucified Jesus in his hands, feet, and side. This incident captures for me the depth of Francis's relationship with God; his was such an intense prayer life that God gifted him with the stigmata. Francis challenged us always to be in a relationship with God, especially through prayer.

Another earlier incident took place one day as he prayed before the crucifix in the tumbledown chapel of San Damiano, outside the city walls of Assisi. Francis heard Jesus whisper from the crucifix, "Francis, rebuild my house which you see is falling into ruins." Francis at San Damiano challenged us to build up our households, our parish community and beyond. How? By doing good. Seize the day.

A third incident is Francis's encounter with a leper. As Francis rode on horseback one day, a man with leprosy appeared. Francis started to ride away. But no! Francis slowly dismounted and embraced the leper. He saw in that leper the brokenness of human beings. We may want to get away, as Francis was tempted, to avoid distressing situations. Francis's embrace of the leper challenges us as well. There are many ways to become healers, peacemakers, and comforters. All we have to do is "just do it."

This planet of ours, in many ways, hasn't changed much since the days of Francis in the thirteenth century. It's dysfunctional.

La Verna, San Damiano, and the leper are three incidents that show Francis was able to cut through the trivia of human life and focus on three essential questions: our relationship with God; our relationships with one another, especially family; and our positive, proactive response to the brokenness in our fellow human beings and ourselves.

So I believe our Pope Francis chose his name well. May these events and more in the life of Saint Francis, whose feast day we celebrate, inspire us to intensify our own prayer lives, to build up our families, and to reach out with helping hands to the people all around us. May his prayers be carved deeply into the core of our own being.

Twenty-Eighth Sunday in Ordinary Time

I just read about a woman who went to an artist to ask him to paint her portrait.

When the portrait was done, the painter asked whether she liked it. She said, "No. It's missing something. Diamonds." So the painter added diamonds to the portrait everywhere. Pretty soon she was glittering with diamonds from head to toe. "That's me," she said. And she bought the portrait.

The painter said, "I have had many unusual requests, but yours is the most unusual. Why all these diamonds in your portrait?"

The woman, in her seventies, answered, "I'm afraid I'm going to heaven before my husband, and he'll probably try to remarry a high school sweetheart. And if he does, I want her to kill herself looking for these diamonds."

So much for gems.

Here's a true story about three high school students who grew up in poor, broken homes in Newark, New Jersey; and in a neighborhood riddled with crime, drugs, and violence. One day these students heard about a program in medicine for minority students and made what they came to call "The Pact."

They agreed that together they would apply for this program; together they would graduate from college, and together they would finish medical school and come back to practice in Newark.

The three were accepted into the program. In college they stuck together in a very different academic environment. They prodded, pushed, and supported each other. They studied together, worked summer jobs together, and yes, they partied together. They learned how to solve problems together.

Two made it to medical school, and the third went to dental school. Despite their different schedules, they continued to stick together.

In their ten-year odyssey, there were times when they wanted to give up on their dreams and times when they made bad decisions. But because of the power of their friendship, The Pact endured, and their dreams came true. These three doctors wrote a best-selling book titled *The Pact*.

Now the incredible journey of these three began when they had the intuition to see the possibilities within one another. And Jesus in today's Gospel recognized the potential for spiritual greatness in the wealthy young man. And I hope that each one of you recognizes the potential for greatness within yourselves and your families and friends. Yes, I hope recognition for greatness will impel us to help one another realize the incredible potential for good we all have.

Now the word of God for today takes us back to the wisdom literature of ancient Israel. The author pleads not for wealth, power, celebrity, health, or beauty but for true wisdom that will enable us to distinguish what's important in life; this is the wisdom that will enable us to answer the fundamental questions of human life: Who am I? What am I living for? And what is the ultimate purpose of my life? Yes, pray that God will grace us with true wisdom.

The author of the letter to the Hebrews we heard today spoke about the word of God, which, like a surgical knife, can open us up and reveal our true selves: either other centered toward God and our fellow human beings or self-centered.

The author asked you and me the following: What drives our lives? God and our fellow human beings? Or our own self-seeking?

And in the Gospel according to Mark we have the story of the energetic, well-to-do young man who wasn't content with his life. He was looking for something more. He wanted eternal life. And, oh yes, he had observed all the commandments.

But he wanted to know what else he should do. And Jesus recognized the potential for spiritual greatness within him and said, "You are lacking in one thing. Go, sell what you have, and give to [the] poor...then come, follow me." (Mark 10:21) But sadly this young man couldn't give up what he had, couldn't see the potential for spiritual greatness within himself.

Yes, this young man was searching for fuller and deeper meaning. The so-called good life didn't seem to satisfy him. He wanted to live for something more, for someone greater than himself. And this is indeed the quest of so many people.

A well-known author Viktor Frankl was an inmate of Hitler's concentration camp at Dachau, just outside of Munich in Germany. Among the books he authored is *Man's Search for Meaning*.

In prewar Vienna, Frankl had a wife, two children, a good psychiatric profession, and a comfortable home. But he lost all these. In the concentration camp of Adolph Hitler, he lost every earthly thing he treasured—wife, children, profession, and home. And these losses brought him face-to-face with the fundamental questions of human life: Who really am I? What should I be living for? And what is the ultimate purpose of my earthly life?

Frankl discovered in the concentration camp that people could put up with incredible hardships, cruelties, and sufferings without losing their serenity and respect for others, provided they saw that these hardships had some ultimate meaning.

In their hearts, people yearn for something or someone beyond themselves who can give greater meaning and value to their lives. And this something else or someone else can take different forms, such as family, a profession, a passion for justice, the greater common good, and so forth. When a person finds something that gives transcendent meaning to his or her existence, that meaning awakens new energies within that person. He or she sees more, performs better, and in short becomes a man or woman of faith.

Every man or woman of faith has some God to whom he or she gives ultimate allegiance. That object may be something quite finite—wealth or power as in today's Gospel—or it may be God himself, the absolute good. The novelist Fyodor Dostoevsky wrote in *The Brothers Karamazov*, "Every man, every woman, must bend his or her knee before some god."

You and I profess to find the ultimate meaning of life in Jesus, who by the power of the Spirit invites us to see in Jesus the very face of God.

We recognize the presence of God in the signs he has given to us, the community of believers, in the sacramental life of this community: water, bread, wine, and oil. We reach out in love and compassion to one another. Eventually we let go of this earthly life in the mystery of death so we can be transformed into a new, heavenly reality.

Jesus in this Gospel recognized the potential for spiritual greatness in the wealthy young man and, when asked, gave him a pathway. But that young man walked away. Consider again the incredible journey of three New Jersey high schoolers who had the intuition to see the possibilities within each other; they joined together in a pact, supporting each other in a new direction.

I hope each one of you recognizes the potential for greatness within yourselves and your families and friends. I hope that recognition will impel us to help one another realize the incredible potential for good we all have.

Twenty-Ninth Sunday in Ordinary Time

I heard a story about two teaching nuns who were shopping at a supermarket on a 100-degree-plus day. As they passed by the beer cooler, one nun said to the other, "Wouldn't a nice cool beer be refreshing?"

The second nun answered, "Indeed, but I wouldn't feel comfortable buying beer, since I'm sure someone would recognize us at the checkout counter."

"I can handle it," the other nun replied, picking up a six-pack and heading for the checkout.

The cashier looked surprised. "We use beer for washing our hair," the nun explained. "Back at our convent, we call it 'Catholic shampoo.'"

Without blinking an eye, the cashier placed a bag of pretzels with the beer. He looked the nun in the eye and said, "Pretzels to set your hair when you wash it with beer."

Now that's what I call a witty response.

The word of God takes us back in our imaginations to the sixth century before Jesus (the 500s) to the second section of the book of Isaiah (a.k.a. Deutero-Isaiah).

This is one of the so-called servant songs. The author portrayed an innocent servant who suffered and died so others could have life. The early Christians saw in this song the saving work of Jesus Christ. God became one of us in Jesus so we might be in a relationship with God forever. The word of God may be asking us whether we nurture this relationship, especially in prayer.

The author of the letter to the Hebrews spoke about a great high priest, Jesus Christ, completely divine and yet completely human like ourselves. Through his horrific death and glorious resurrection, he reestablished our relationship with God. Do we realize, the author may be asking, that prayer is at the heart of Christianity because at the heart of Christianity is our relationship with God?

And in the Gospel according to Mark, we have two disciples arguing over the privilege of status in the age to come without realizing the cost of discipleship. Jesus asked, "Can you drink the cup that I drink?" That is, can you drink the cup of suffering? And then Jesus concluded that to be a disciple means to serve others. Serving others, not lording over others, is exercising leadership in our community of disciples.

Today I would like to reflect on the mystery of suffering in light of the word of God. Within the mystery of suffering is a spiritual power that can draw us more closely to Jesus Christ and transform us into sharers in God's eternal life, because hidden within the mystery of Jesus's suffering was the glory of his resurrection. Our Christian faith proclaims that hidden in every Good Friday is an Easter hope or joy. Think about it.

Someone in a family, for example, loses a job, is diagnosed with a serious illness, sees a relationship beginning to unravel, or realizes that a loved one has a chemical addiction. And then together this family tries, as best it can, to deal with this "cross" and thereby bring hope, healing, forgiveness—and resurrection—to their life together.

Yes, the love that binds a family together can transform every tragic and desperate Good Friday into an Easter hope. Or a student can't understand the numbers and diagrams in the algebra text. This student is lost and discouraged, and wants to quit. And a teacher wants to go home after a long week; but, seeing the student's frustration, the teacher puts down a pile of books and papers, and patiently walks through the problems with the befuddled student. And after a lot of hard work and patience, the lights come on for that student. That teacher's selfless caring and generous gift of time transformed that student's Good Friday into Easter light.

Or a working mother has lost all of her accrued vacation and leave time to care for her seriously ill child. She is about to lose her job—and the important medical benefits. And then her coworkers devise a plan to pool some of their vacation time and cover her responsibilities so she can keep her job and benefits while caring for her sick child. Those coworkers transformed a mother's Good Friday of desperation into an Easter of possibility.

The point is simple. We sometimes find ourselves stuck in a situation; our problems sometimes batter and even overwhelm us. In such moments, our faith challenges us to remember that good will ultimately conquer evil, that love transforms hate, that light shatters darkness. The ministry of Jesus didn't end in the tragedy of the cross but in the triumph of the resurrection. Yes, hidden within the mystery of his suffering is the glory of his resurrection, eternal life.

As I reflect on suffering, I can't help but think of the story told by Elie Wiesel in his book *Night*, a memoir of his experiences at the Auschwitz and Buchenwald concentration camps. He described how the SS marched all the inmates to the parade grounds and there hanged a youngster as a warning to the other inmates not to try an escape. And as the youngster hung there dying, Elie Wiesel, a youngster himself, heard a voice behind him say, "Where is God now?"

This is an eternal question, highlighted in the biblical book of Job, in *The Confessions of St. Augustine*, in the literature of nineteenth-century Russian novelist Fyodor Dostoevsky, and in best sellers today, such as Rabbi Harold Kushner's *When Bad Things Happen to Good People*.

Yes, as we reflect on the human situation, on the Middle East in shambles, on millions of refugees fleeing violence, on senseless shootings in some of our own schools, we realize the entire planet cries out for God's healing grace.

There is, of course, no satisfactory answer to the mystery of suffering and evil. Yes, at times suffering results from sin, immoral behavior, or the misuse of freedom. Autocrats, for example, deny their people basic human rights and cause untold suffering. At other times, suffering results from an unfinished, incomplete universe, a universe in process, to paraphrase Saint Paul's letter to the Romans. But ultimately, suffering is a mystery. How should we respond to it?

First, remember that God is always near us. He is forever bringing us to a fuller life. He will never abandon us. "Can a mother forget her infant...Even should she forget, I will never forget you.'" (Isaiah 49:15)

Second, we ought to remember that the mystery of suffering can have healing and redemptive power. Why? Because Jesus, through the mystery of his own passion in Gethsemane, death on Calvary, and resurrection from the tomb, reestablished that relationship we had at the beginning with God.

Our everyday inescapable "aches and pains," borne with love, can be redemptive and bring forth new life in us and others. That's because the sufferings of Jesus did precisely that: they brought forth resurrection and life for us, for all.

We cannot begin to imagine what life after this earthly life will be like, but we know God will satisfy our deepest longings. Think about it: "eye has not seen, and ear has not heard...what God has prepared for those who love him." (1 Cor. 2:9)

And so on this day, as we reflect on the mystery of suffering in light of the word of God, let us remember that hidden in the sufferings of Jesus on Good Friday was the glory of his resurrection on Easter. We can bring Easter hope to someone's Good Friday by reaching out to him or her with a helping hand, listening ear, or encouraging word.

Thirtieth Sunday in Ordinary Time

Every youngster knows Halloween. If your children or grandchildren go trick or treating, be sure they have a fun and safe time.

You may have heard about the real estate agent who moved his office to a new location. A friend ordered a bouquet of flowers to be delivered.

Well, there was a mix-up. The flowers arrived at the office opening with a note attached reading, "Rest in Peace."

Now the sender was, of course, annoyed. But the real estate agent had a different perspective. "Think of it this way," he said. "Somewhere in town, someone was buried with a bouquet that read, 'Good luck in your new location.'"

The word of God today takes us back to the sixth century before Jesus (the 500s). Jeremiah generally was a prophet of doom and gloom (he saw the collapse of the kingdom of the South), but here Jeremiah spoke about hope, a new beginning for a people, now conquered but soon to be free—now overwhelmed by tragedies but soon to enjoy prosperity and peace.

The book of Jeremiah challenges us to hope always in God, even when bad things happen to us. The author of the letter to the Hebrews speaks about the saving work of Jesus, our high priest, who through his death and resurrection reestablished our broken relationship with God and who, in the mystery of our own dying, will transform us into a new, indescribable, heavenly life.

The author challenged us to see reality in light of our ultimate purpose: a life in a relationship with God forever. One day we, like the risen Jesus, will be transformed, in the mystery of our dying, into a new heavenly life.

And in the Gospel, Jesus asked a blind man, "What do you want me to do for you?" (Mark 10:51) If Jesus asked you and me that question right now, how would we answer?

The blind man answered, "I want to see."

And Jesus said, "Your faith has saved you." And the blind man did see.

Today I would like to reflect briefly on a book that nurtures the faith that saves us: the Bible. But how do we understand or interpret the Bible so it nurtures our faith?

A while ago a friend answered the doorbell and found a young man with a Bible in his hand. This young man had clear, definite, black-and-white answers to life's complex questions. He was a biblical fundamentalist,

How do fundamentalists differ from mainstream Catholics? We do agree about certain beliefs—for example, that Jesus is a God-man (the mystery of the incarnation), was born of the Virgin Mary, and reestablished our relationship with God through his death and resurrection. Moreover, media preachers often shout, "Back to the basics; just the fundamentals, please." Fundamentalism, by the way, cuts across all major monotheistic faiths; there are Jewish fundamentalists, Christian fundamentalists, and Muslim fundamentalists.

Mainstream Catholics and biblical fundamentalists disagree in their approach to the Bible—in other words, how they interpret the Bible. Fundamentalists say God dictated every word in the Bible and believe that every word in the Bible is to be understood literally.

Catholics recognize that the biblical writers, in light of their culture, used various forms of communication or literary forms (for example, poetry, drama, historical narrative, fiction, and so forth) to communicate certain religious truths about God, the universe, and ourselves. And just as we interpret literary genres differently today, so too must we interpret biblical literary genres.

The writers didn't communicate scientific truths. We say, for example, that the sun rises or sets at a particular hour. Actually the sun doesn't rise or set, so we first must know what kind of literary genre the writers were using. Then we will be able to discover more easily the fundamental religious truth the literary genre is trying to communicate. And the Bible often speaks symbolically—for example, the parables of Jesus aren't to be understood literally.

The two creation stories in the Bible communicate certain truths: God is the absolute Creator, everything God made is good, evil comes from human sin, men and women are equal in dignity, and so forth. The literary form the ancient writer chose derived from the Babylonian culture with which he was familiar.

For mainstream Catholics, the Bible is a privileged form of God's communication to us—a two-way communication between God and us. And that is why we have to prayerfully search for God's voice in the Bible. What in particular are some of the challenges Catholics face in conversations with biblical fundamentalists? Let me highlight two:

First, fundamentalists say, "Why don't Catholics see the Bible as simply the word of God? Why do they require the authority of the church to know religious truths?" The Bible isn't always easily understandable; in fact, it's sometimes open to different interpretations. The authority of the church authentically interprets the Bible.

Yes, the church is a biblical community in the sense that it acknowledges and proclaims the Bible as the privileged word of God in human form. The New Testament, in particular, points to Jesus of Nazareth as the unique revelation of God to us. Everything God ever wanted to do or say to us he did and said in Jesus of Nazareth. That is why the church believes there will be no new revealer or revelation.

The Spirit guides the church universal in interpreting Jesus Christ, our way, our truth, and our life in every generation and in every culture. Redemption or salvation is a gift or grace from God by virtue of the death and resurrection of Jesus and the outpouring of the Spirit.

Second, why does the church repeat the sacrifice of the Mass? Didn't Jesus die once and for all outside the walls of the old Jerusalem? Yes. That's the one and only sacrifice. But at the Last Supper, Jesus said, "Do this in memory of me." We experience again the one saving sacrifice of Jesus at every Mass until Jesus Christ comes again in glory.

The Eucharist, called the Mass, is a sacrifice, a sacrificial meal, in the sense that it makes present again for us, at different times and in different places, the redemptive, salvific activity of Jesus Christ on the cross.

The Mass is in no way a separate sacrifice from the cross. Through certain signs entrusted to the church universal, the community of believers, made up of saints and sinners—entrusted with signs such as water in baptism, bread and wine in the Eucharist, oil in confirmation, and the healing of the sick—communicates the living Christ's life and grace to us.

And so what can we learn from biblical fundamentalists? Love for the scriptures, enthusiasm for proclaiming the word of God, the need we all have for relationships or friendships with God and our fellow human beings, as well as peace of mind in an increasingly life-threatening planet.

May the Bible, the word of God in human form, a privileged form of God's communication to us, nurture our faith. And may our faith save us, just as it saved the blind man in today's Gospel.

All Saints

You may have heard the story about Father Murphy, known
affectionately as Murph. Parishioners loved him. He was a wonderful
human being. But as a preacher, he was forgetful, rambling, and repetitive.
Often he didn't seem to know where he was going in his homilies. Word
got back to the bishop, Murph's classmate.

The bishop decided to give Murph a few homily pointers. The bishop said, "You have to grab the congregation's attention. For example, last weekend I began: 'I'm in love with a woman.' A hush in the congregation. 'I've been in love with her for forty years.' Another hush in the congregation. 'That woman is the Virgin Mary, the Mother of God.'"

Next Sunday, Father Murphy began his homily, announcing, "The bishop is in love with a woman." Shock waves. "For forty years." More shock. "But for the life of me," said Murph, "I can't remember her name." So much for memory.

The word of God takes us back in our imaginations to the book of Revelation (a.k.a. the Apocalypse). This literary genre, popular between 200 BC and AD 100, contains symbolic figures, visions, numbers, colors, and animals. It is not easily understandable and definitely not to be understood literally.

There are three basic scenes in this last book of the Bible: a message to seven churches; a heavenly liturgy, in which the slain Lamb, Jesus Christ, approaches the throne of God and breaks open the scrolls, which predict the End Times; and the final scene or conflict between the woman and the dragon, between angelic forces and satanic forces. The author pled to the persecuted Christians, "Stay the course. Good ultimately will triumph over evil."

In this particular vision, a huge number of people (the elect) gather around the throne of God. The white robes symbolize their baptism; the palm branches, their victory over death; and the lamb, Jesus Christ, our redeemer. And all gathered sing out, "Salvation comes from our God, who is seated on the throne, and from the Lamb." (Rev. 7:10)

You and I pray that we will be counted in that heavenly life Saint Paul described so eloquently in his letter to the Christian community at Corinth: "eye has not seen, and ear has not heard...what God has prepared for those who love him." (1 Cor. 2:9)

The letter of John proclaims that we are sons and daughters of God, that we shall be like God, and that we shall see God as he is. We ask that this awesome future will be ours: to see God as God is.

And in the Gospel according to Matthew, Jesus described the meaning of discipleship: they recognize who they are (fragile creatures in the presence of an awesome Creator), and they hunger for God in their daily lives. They forgive wrongs done to them; they, like the Virgin Mary, have God's will as their first priority. They are peacemakers; and yes, they are ready to suffer rather than betray the Master. What a splendid spirituality for you and me: the beatitudes, which so many saints lived out and so many people today are living.

Occasionally I watch the Academy Awards. One of the most inspiring moments for me was the presentation of a special lifetime achievement Oscar to Sidney Poitier. In a career that spanned more than fifty years, Poitier appeared in some forty films, including *Guess Who's Coming to Dinner, A Raisin in the Sun,* and *In the Heat of the Night.* In his eloquent acceptance speech, Poitier deflected attention away from his own accomplishments. He said, in so many words, that he arrived in Hollywood at a time when the odds against an African American standing here would not have fallen in his favor…if there were not a handful of visionary filmmakers who were not afraid to reflect their values, ethical and moral. And Poitier gave thanks to those who went before him and "altered the odds" and made his life's work possible.

My good people, we, too, should be grateful to God, especially in November as we remember the faithful departed. Yes, we are grateful for those who have gone before us and on whose shoulders we stand, so to speak, those who have made our lives possible, including our parents and grandparents, a teacher or relative, or a mentor or friend.

In particular, we should be grateful for the faith community to which we belong and which gives noble purpose to our lives. But why should we be grateful to God for our community, which is made up of so many saints, whose feast day we celebrate. Let me give you a few good reasons:

1. We are a worldwide community of believers (one billion plus of rich and poor, black and white, American, European, Asian, and African), a family that celebrates the presence of the living Christ in the liturgies of the word and the Eucharist, where the bread and wine become sacramentally the reality of Jesus Christ. Yes, we are a worldwide community of believers who possess within ourselves the spark of the divine, a flame we should never let go out.

2. We are a community with splendid heroes and heroines. We are the Church of Francis and Clare of Assisi, Anthony of Padua, Ignatius Loyola, Thomas More, Teresa of Avila, Vincent de Paul, Therese of Lisieux, Padre Pio, Mother Teresa, and the litany goes on. These are people worth imitating in our own quest for ultimate meaning.

3. We are a community that always has something to celebrate: the blessing of animals in October, the communion of saints today, Our Lady of Guadalupe in December, Saint Nicholas in Advent, Christmas, Ash Wednesday, Easter, Pentecost, and the great feasts of the Virgin Mary.

4. We are a community that takes a stand on peace and justice. The Catholic community sponsors and staffs countless shelters, hospices, soup kitchens, battered-women's shelters, AIDS treatment, literacy programs, day care centers, hospitals, and schools throughout the world. And hundreds of Catholic relief and refugee agencies attempt to meet the basic needs of the poor.

But alas, we are also a community of believers with tensions, because we are made up of human beings. And not everyone is as good as we would like. Some people are dysfunctional, messy, and make a mess out of their lives and the lives of others. So we have to live with some messiness and muddle through as best we can.

Today, the feast of all saints invites us to give thanks to God: for parents and grandparents, relatives and mentors and friends, heroes and heroines. And if they are deceased, remember them in prayer, especially during this month of November. Perhaps you may drive to the cemetery, if they are close by, to honor them.

Above all, give thanks for the faith community to which we belong, a community that calls us to be in a relationship with God here on this planet, for that is the purpose of life: to be in a relationship with God here and beyond our earthly lives. Yes, be proud and grateful to belong to this worldwide community.

Thirty-Second Sunday in Ordinary Time

The baseball season is finally over. My poor beloved New York Mets....

As a youngster, I wanted to be a baseball pitcher. One day the little league coach approached me on the mound and said, "I think I better have someone else relieve you."

I argued, "I struck this guy out last time."

"Yes, I know," said the coach, "but it's still the same inning. He's at bat again." And so ended my baseball-pitching career.

A parishioner told me to be brief in light of the festival. He reminded me that the Ten Commandments are only 297 words; the Bill of Rights, 463 words; and Lincoln's Gettysburg Address, just 266 words. But I reminded him that a federal directive on the price of cabbage ran almost 27,000 words. So, I guess my homily can be longer than the Gettysburg Address.

The word of God takes us back in our imaginations to the ninth century before Jesus, the 800s, to a Hebrew prophet named Elijah. Here a widow, a non-Jew or so-called Gentile, was down to her last handful of flour and a tiny bit of oil. She encountered Elijah, who asked for a cup of water and a bit of bread. She explains her shortage, but Elijah said to her, "Do not be afraid. Go and do as you have said. But first make me a little cake and bring it to me. Afterwards you can prepare something for yourself and your son." (1 Kings 17:12-13)

The widow faced a dilemma: Should she trust in Elijah's God who, Elijah says, would provide a never-ending supply of flour and oil?

Or should she feed her starving child first? Trust in Elijah's God and hospitality won out. And miraculously, the prophet's promise came true. She had a never-ending supply. That truly was a great act of faith in God's providence. This word challenges us to trust always in God and to be hospitable to one another.

And in the Gospel, we heard a similar story about a widow who put her last two coins, a small sum, into the temple treasury in Jerusalem. Jesus commented that, in contrast to those who gave from their surplus, this woman gave "her whole livelihood." This too was a great act of faith in God's providence. This word challenged us to "trust in God" and to be generous with what we have.

The author of Hebrews spoke about the superiority of Jesus's one sacrifice compared to the many sacrifices in the temple of Jerusalem. Through his death and resurrection, Jesus opened up eternal life to humankind, an indescribable heavenly life beyond this earthly life.

As I thought about the two poor women in today's word of God, I remembered a newspaper photographer sharing a simple, compassionate scene after a devastating earthquake in Latin America. A long line of people waited for food. At the very end stood a girl of about twelve years of age. Finally, the only thing left was one lonely banana. She took the precious gift and ran across the street, where three small children waited: perhaps her sisters and a brother. She divided the banana into three equal parts to feed the three youngsters and then licked the inside of that banana peel. "In that moment I swear I saw the face of God!" wrote the photographer.

Yes, the young girl revealed the "face of God" to this photographer and perhaps others. And isn't that what life should be all about? Yes, the word of God challenges us to ask ourselves, do we reveal the face of God to one another?

As disciples of Jesus, we too ought to show the face of God in our everyday behavior, especially by living the beatitudes Matthew summed up so splendidly in chapter 5 of his Gospel. I would like to think Jesus would say this about us.

If you're working to pay the bills but making time to be with your children whenever they need you, blessed are you. You may never own a big vacation home and a Lexus, but heaven will be yours.

If you are overwhelmed by the care of a dying spouse, a sick child, or an elderly parent but try your best to make a loving home, blessed are you. One day your sorrow will be transformed into joy.

If you happily give your time to serve at a soup kitchen, shop for the housebound, help a youngster with a classroom assignment; if you befriend the uncool, the unpopular, the lost, blessed are you. Count God among your friends.

If you refuse to take shortcuts when it comes to doing what is right, if you refuse to compromise your integrity and ethics, and if you refuse to rationalize that "everyone does it," blessed are you—you will triumph.

If you try to understand things from the perspective of the other person and find a way to make things work for the good, if you're feeling discouraged and frustrated because you are paying the price for loving the unlovable and forgiving the undeserving, blessed are you. God will welcome, forgive, and love you.

If you readily spend time listening to and consoling; if you manage to heal wounds and build bridges; if others see in you goodness, graciousness, joy, and serenity; if you can see the good in everyone and seek the good for everyone, blessed are you. You are nothing less than the face of God in our midst.

"Rejoice and be glad," Jesus said; you are the blessed of God. In the end heaven is yours.

May God give each one of us the grace to show the face of God to one another: yes, the way the beatitudes in Matthew 5 call us to, the way the two poor women in the word of God did, and the way that twelve-year-old girl showed the face of God to that photographer. Heaven will be yours.

Thirty-Third Sunday in Ordinary Time

I read that Bill O'Reilly's best seller *Killing Reagan* has generated controversy for being fast and loose with facts. One thing for sure about Ronald Reagan was that he had a sense of humor. Here is one of my favorite Reagan stories.

The parents of five-year-old twins, worried that the boys were developing extreme personalities (one a pessimist, the other an optimist), took them to a psychiatrist. The psychiatrist showed the pessimist a room full of toys. The little boy burst into tears.

"What's the matter?" the psychiatrist asked. "Don't you want to play with the toys?"

"Yes," the little boy bawled, "but I don't see my favorite toy."

Next the psychiatrist took the optimist to a room piled to the ceiling with the stuff you find on the floor of a horse stable. The optimist yelled with delight and began digging.

"What do you think you're doing?" the psychiatrist asked.

"With all this manure," the little boy said, beaming, "there must be a pony here somewhere!"

The point? Reagan was always looking for the "pony" in all the bad stuff that ended up on his desk. What is the moral of the story? Be an optimist.

You may wonder why today's word of God is about gloom and doom.

The liturgical year celebrates the story of our salvation. The liturgical cycle begins in Advent, where we await the Messiah; then it moves to the birth of the Messiah at Christmas. Then it goes on to Lent, where we focus on the three-age-old traditions: prayer, fasting or doing without, and almsgiving or charitable works. Next we enter into the chief week of the liturgical year—Holy Week—with Palm Sunday or the entrance of Jesus into Jerusalem, his Last Supper, and his horrific sacrificial death and glorious resurrection—a dying and rising, which re-established our relationship with God. We re-experience the outpouring of the Spirit anew at Pentecost. And the cycle then continues throughout Sundays in ordinary time, when we walk the roadways of Galilee and Judea with Jesus as he works signs and wonders, proclaiming that the kingdom of God is breaking into our lives.

This liturgical cycle culminates in the final coming of Jesus Christ in glory. Next Sunday, on the feast of Christ, the King, we reach the end of salvation history when every human being and all that is will be subjected to Christ, "when he hands over the kingdom to his God and Father." (1Cor 15:24)

Yes, in the annual liturgical cycle we celebrate the story that began on the first page of scripture: "In the beginning God created the heavens and the earth." We finally reach a story that ends on the last page of scripture: "Come, Lord Jesus." Yes, God will transform this universe into his glorious kingdom in all its fullness, and that is why we proclaim in the eucharistic prayer, "Christ has died; Christ is risen; Christ will come again." How this universe as we know it will end (whether in fire or ice, as Robert Frost says in his remarkable poem), we don't know. But how it will end isn't the question. Rather the question is, are we ready to meet the living Christ when he comes to us in the mystery of death? One thing is certain: we will die.

The book of Daniel takes us back to a crisis in second-century Judaism. Greek oppressors were doing everything they could to force the Jews to give up their biblical faith in God and deny their covenantal relationship with God. In a visionary experience, Daniel pled, in effect, don't give up your faith despite the cruelties you're enduring; stand your ground. The archangel Michael will protect you; God will win out and you will shine brightly. Yes, good ultimately will triumph over evil. The word challenges us to persevere in our lives of discipleship with Jesus despite the everyday doubts we may have about the nearness of God's presence to us, especially if things are going badly.

The author of the letter to the Hebrews recalled the one sacrifice of Jesus. Through his horrific death and glorious resurrection, Jesus re-established our relationship with God. The word challenges us to grow in that relationship with God by living out a life of discipleship with Jesus.

And in the Gospel according to Mark, Jesus spoke about an apocalypse, a cosmic upheaval: a darkened sun, an unlit moon, falling stars—all symbolic and scary images. Yes, Jesus Christ will usher in the glorious kingdom of God in all its fullness. The Gospel author urged us to always be ready to meet the living Christ, because we don't know when he actually will come to us in the mystery of death. The word asks whether we are ready now to meet the living Christ. And if not today, when?

You may have read Rabbi Harold Kushner's best seller *When Bad Things Happen to Good People*. It's about the problem of evil. Why do wicked appear to prosper and good suffer? It's a twenty-first-century version of the biblical book of Job. Kushner published another book *Living a Life that Matters*.

Kushner writes that in his forty years as a rabbi, he has cared for many people in the last moments of their lives. The people who had the most trouble with death were those who felt they had never done anything worthwhile. And if God would only give them another two or three years, maybe they would finally get it right. Death didn't frighten them; no, what frightened them was the fear that they would die and leave no mark on the world. They judged they had made no difference for the better in the lives of other people.

We shouldn't be frightened that God will end the world as we know it. What we're really called to do is to begin bringing about the end of this world as Jesus did in his ministry: by having our priorities straight—seeking God in our everyday lives; by being peacemakers; by treating one another fairly; by helping people know they have a purpose in life; and by giving a helping hand to the people whose lives touch ours every day, especially the neglected, depressed, and lonely.

Let me close with a true story about a violinist who tripped and fell as he went on stage to play for a special concert in Helsinki, Finland. He almost went into shock when the priceless Stradivarius in his hand broke into several pieces. But a master craftsman spent hours putting it back together. And afterward, the violin seemed to play better than before.

This illustrates something that can happen to any one of us. Sometimes our lives can break into pieces. But we can pick up the pieces of our lives and let the master craftsman—Jesus Christ—put our lives back together so we can become the generous hands, compassionate eyes, hopeful voice, and dedicated feet of Jesus to one another until he comes again with great power and glory at the End Times.

Today's word of God fixes our eyes on Christ's final coming "with great power and glory." (Mark 13:26) But it would be a tragedy for us if that vision or horizon blinded us to the here and now, where we can be the generous hands, compassionate eyes, hopeful voices, and dedicated feet of Jesus to the people who touch our lives every day.

Feast of Christ the King

I begin with a story about a medieval knight who returned to his castle one day with his face bruised and badly swollen. His armor was dented, the plume on his helmet was broken, and his horse was limping. The lord of the castle asked, "What happened to you?"

The knight replied, "I've been fighting for you all day: bloodying and pillaging your enemies in the west."

The astonished lord gasped. "But I don't have any enemies to the west."

"Oh," said the knight. "I think you do now."

What is the moral of the story? Know who your friends are.

Next Thursday, we celebrate the Thanksgiving story—a remarkable narrative about people who never gave up on their dreams. Think about it. In September 1620, about 120 men, women, and children (plus crew) set sail from Plymouth, England, on a rickety 113-foot-long ship known as the *Mayflower*. They crossed the treacherous Atlantic and anchored off a spot they named Plymouth, Massachusetts. These so-called pilgrims suffered a bitter winter, in which half of them died from disease, hunger, and cold. But they persevered in their quest for their four freedoms: freedom of speech, freedom of worship, freedom from want, and freedom from fear.

One year after their arrival, in 1621, they celebrated a great feast of Thanksgiving to God for their survival and harvest of plenty. And so this Thanksgiving, I invite all of us to give thanks to God for our many blessings—family, friends, freedoms, and the opportunities we have to realize our dreams.

Today we celebrate the feast of Christ, the King, the One to whom we owe our ultimate allegiance, the One who is the image of the invisible God, the One through whom we have a relationship with the triune God.

Now the word *king* evokes many images. The pomp and circumstance at Buckingham Palace; or Shakespeare's *King Lear*, old and foolish and mad. Or we may think of the overly passionate King David of ancient Israel, the not-so-wise King Solomon, the extravagant King Louis XIV of France, or some of the ceremonial monarchs in our twenty-first century. And yes, a few youngsters may think of Burger King. Whatever image of king comes to mind may influence our thoughts about today's feast.

What is the feast of Christ, the King about? And why at the end of the liturgical year?

Christ, the King fits appropriately into the liturgical cycle, which begins with Advent or the hope for a Messiah, then Christmas with the Messiah's birth, then to the dying and rising of Jesus at Easter, and finally, after the Sundays in ordinary time, to the end of the liturgical cycle, when Jesus Christ comes in great glory and power in today's feast of Christ, the King.

In this feast, we reach the end of salvation history as we understand it, where (to paraphrase Saint Paul) Jesus Christ will hand over the kingdom of heaven—a kingdom of truth, life, love, holiness, grace, peace, and justice—to God, our Father.

The word of God today takes us back to the second century before Jesus (the 100s). The author of the book of Daniel wanted to inspire hope in the Jews who are suffering cruelties because of their biblical faith in God. In particular, the author described a visionary experience at the end of human history, where the forces of good and evil will engage in a final apocalyptic struggle. In the midst of this struggle appeared the figure of a mysterious "son of man," who came upon the clouds of heaven. And this mysterious figure went before the throne of God, the Ancient One, who brought about his definitive reign through the kingship of this mysterious "son of man." The Christians saw this in this figure Jesus Christ.

The passage from the book of Revelation speaks to Christians in the first century, who also were suffering cruelties because of their faith in God. Jesus, once dead and now gloriously alive, re-established that relationship between God and us. He is the Alpha and the Omega, the beginning and the end, the One who is, was, and is to come, the Almighty One.

And in the Gospel according to John, Pilate asked political questions: whether Jesus was heir to the throne of Israel and possibly a threat to Rome. But Jesus turned the table on Pilate, saying the term *kingdom* had to be understood differently. His kingdom was neither political nor despotic. He wouldn't challenge the emperor of Rome. Jesus's kingdom was at one and the same time within and beyond us. Jesus witnessed to this. He is the truth and the way to the truth. He is life and the way to life. Yes, God, always faithful and reliable, will bring about his redemptive purpose in human history through Jesus by the power of the Spirit despite human resistance.

Now it is to Jesus that we owe our allegiance. But do we? It is said that the way we use our time, talents, and resources usually indicates who and what we prize most. Someone, for example, may say, "I enjoy reading novels." But to the question "When did you last read a novel?" he or she may answer, "Five years ago?" Then reading novels isn't actually a high value for that person.

We as a faith community say we give our ultimate allegiance to Jesus Christ. We say we prize Jesus most in our lives. But then we might ask ourselves, how do we spend our time? With Jesus in prayer and in service to others? Or are we simply absorbed in ourselves, a what's-in-it-for-me attitude? We've heard the quote often enough, attributed to Stephen Grellet: "I shall pass through this world but once: any good therefore that I can do or any kindness that I can show to any human being, let me do it now, let me not defer or neglect it, for I shall not pass this way again."

The great nineteenth-century Russian novelist, Fyodor Dostoevsky, wrote in his classic *The Brothers Karamazov* that every man or woman of faith wants to believe in someone or something that is ultimately true.

We confess and proclaim that Jesus is our life and our truth. But is he? What motivates us? Moves us? What makes us tick? What would Jesus do?

So today we might ask ourselves, how can we pledge ever more deeply our absolute allegiance to Jesus as our Lord? How can we know him better? How can we better sustain that relationship? Yes, how can our relationship with God become such a priority in our lives that in the mystery of our own dying, we can rise with Jesus Christ forever into a new, indescribable, heavenly life?

On this feast of Christ, the King, which concludes our liturgical year, may God empower us to rededicate ourselves to Jesus Christ—our way, truth, and life. And may God continue to bless us abundantly as we express gratitude to God for all our blessings, especially the gift of family, friends, colleagues, and one another.

Endnotes/Citations

Myra Brooks Welch, "The Touch of the Master's Hand," *The Gospel Messenger*, Brethren Press, 1921

Marian Wright Edelman, *Lanterns: A Memoir of Mentors*, Beacon Press, 1999

Holy Father Pope Francis, *Amoris Laetitia (Love in the Family)*, www.vatican.va

BBC News, "Titanic 'crow's nest key' auction," Sept. 5, 2007

Elie Wiesel, *The Town Beyond the Wall: A Novel*, Atheneum, 1964

Paul M. Miller, *The World's Greatest Collection of Church Jokes*, Barbour Publishing Inc., 2013

Marvin Maupin, *It's Better to Die Laughing then to be Dead Serious*, AuthorHouse, 2010

Marcelle Boren, *Disorder in the American Courts*, Iwahu Publishing, 2016

David Heller, *Dear God: Children's Letters to God*, Perigee Trade, 1994

March of the Penguins, DVD, 2005

Stuart George, "Obituary of Common Sense," BBC Radio Stoke (modified, original theme by Lori Borgman, author of *The Death of Common Sense and Profiles of Those Who Knew Him*, Good Cheer Publishing, 2012

Blessed John Henry Newman, "Hope in God-Creator (God has created me to do Him some definite service)," 1848

Erma Bombeck, If Life is a Bowl of Cherries What Am I Doing in the Pits?, Fawcett, 1985

Chariots of Fire, DVD, 2005

Godspell, DVD, 2000

Viktor Frankl, *Man's Search for Meaning*, Beacon Press, 2014

A Raisin in the Sun, DVD, 2000

Warren Bennis, *Learning to Lead: A Workbook on Becoming a Leader*, Basic Books, 2010

Stephen R. Covey, *The 8th Habit: From Effectiveness to Greatness*, Simon & Schuster Ltd., 2006

Robert K. Greenleaf, *The Servant as Religious Leader*, Windy Row, 1983

Pope Francis, *Laudato Si*, www.vatican.va

Abraham Joshua Heschel, *I Asked for Wonder: A Spiritual Anthology*, The Crossroad Publishing Company, 1983

Bob Greene, "When Jordan Cried Behind Closed Doors," *Chicago Tribune*, May 15, 1991

Atul Gawande, *Being Mortal: Medicine and What Matters in the End*, Metropolitan Books, 2014

Blessed John Henry Newman, "The Pillar of the Cloud (Lead, Kindly Light)," 1833

Harold S. Kushner, *When Bad Things Happen to Good People*, Anchor, 2004

Made in the USA
Middletown, DE
27 March 2017